California Cookbook Company Presents

RushHour RECIPES

Compiled by
**Professional Home Economics Teachers
& Family and Consumer Science Teachers
of California, Nevada, Arizona, and Utah**

Editor
Gerry Murry Henderson

Graphic Design, Typography, and Production
Mike Burk Production Services, Long Beach, CA

Visit us on the World Wide Web at:
www.californiacookbook.com

Library of Congress Catalog
Card No. 83-072759
ISBN 0-914159-21-6

1/125M062005/MBPS/DPS

RushHour RECIPES

Thank you for purchasing **Rush Hour Recipes**. *This helps support vital school programs in California, Nevada, Utah, Arizona and Oregon.*

Each recipe has been generously donated by Home Economics and Family and Consumer Science Teachers. We hope that this book helps you prepare delicious recipes when time is of the essence.

We have many people to thank for their part in producing this book and getting it distributed to hundreds of schools:

Grady Reed has been the owner and creator of California Cookbooks for over 25 years. His vision, inspiration and leadership have set a professional standard in cookbooks and fundraising. It has been his attention to detail and absolute dedication to customer service that has made this company what it is today; a provider of quality books and a simple way to raise funds for schools. ***Thank you Grady!***

Nancy Freeman, our office manager for fifteen years, always does her job with a wonderful attitude. She handles customers, salespeople, delivery persons and takes care of all the office details with efficiency and a smile.

Gerry Henderson teaches Home Economics full time at Temple City High School and carefully edits each recipe.

Mike Burk designs our covers and inside photos. He takes the recipes and makes them into the quality books we are so proud of.

Delta Printing, in Valencia, along with **Jerry Bernstein,** makes sure the books are printed professionally and best of all, on time!

Roger Upperman, Robert Mauthe, Ron Rouintree, and **Danny Hawes** organize all the pick-ups of books from our schools and drive thousands of miles to give each teacher great customer service.

Eric Erdmann, Tim Campbell and **Marc Trimble** present these books to students in their classrooms, helping teachers kick off a successful sales drive.

Our photography has been donated by **Hershey Foods, Lawry's Foods, National Cattleman's Beef Association,** and the **National Pork Board.**

As we transition the company to new ownership, we will continue to provide quality cookbooks for the consumer and excellent service to our teachers who work hard to improve their programs.

Sincerely,

Doug Herrema and *Doug Pierce,* owners, California Cookbook Company

P.S. Please note the **re-order form** on page 159.

P.P.S. Please visit us on the web at **www.californiacookbook.com**

Table *of* Contents

California Cookbook
Advisory Committee

KATHIE BACZYNSKI
Mt. Carmel High School, San Diego

PRISCILLA BURNS
Pleasant Valley High School, Chico

JAMIE DAVIS
Redwood Intermediate School, Thousand Oaks

CAROLE DELAP
Golden West High School, Visalia

PEG ELLINGTON
Yucca Valley High School, Yucca Valley

PAM FORD
Temecula Valley High School, Temecula

MARIA FREGULIA
Lassen High School, Susanville

DEBBIE HARVEY
Amador Valley High School, Pleasanton

LA RAE HARGUESS
Hesperia High School

GERRY HENDERSON
Temple City High School, Temple City

GRACE HIBMA
Office of L.A. County Superintendent of Schools,
Consultant Consumer & Homemaking Education

CAMILLE HICKS
Riverton High School, Riverton, UT

NANCY HUNYADI
Fullerton High School, Fullerton

REIKO IKKANDA
So. Pasadena Middle School, So. Pasadena

DOTTI JONES
Etiwanda High School, Etiwanda

MARY LASH
Paramount High School, Paramount

JERI LUNDY
Grossmont High School, La Mesa

JAN MARTIN
Reed High School, Sparks, NV

ANN PORTER
San Luis Obispo High School, San Luis Obispo

BETTY RABIN
Sierra Vista Jr. High School, Canyon Country

APRIL ROSENDAHL
Chino High School, Chino

KAREN TILSON
Poly High School, Riverside

MARIANNE TRAW
Ball Junior High School, Anaheim

SONJA TYREE
Ayala High School, Chino Hills

BETTY WELLS
Bidwell Junior High School, Chico

KATHRYN P. WHITTEN
Home Economics Education, Fresno

iv

Appetizers and Beverages

Artichoke Bruschetta
Serves a crowd

2 French bread baguettes
extra virgin olive oil
1 (small) jar capers
5 cloves garlic, minced
16 Roma tomatoes, chopped
fresh basil leaves, chopped, to taste
1 package artichoke hearts, thawed, chopped
red wine vinegar
salt and pepper, to taste
Parmesan cheese, grated

Slice baguettes into $1/2$" slices and toast on a greased cookie sheet that has been coated with olive oil. Mix jar of capers, juice and all, garlic, tomatoes and basil. Toss chopped artichoke hearts with oil and vinegar. Add to vegetables and mix so bruschetta becomes a salsa. Salt and pepper, to taste. Serve on baguettes topped with grated Parmesan cheese.

Stephanie San Sebastian   Central High School, Fresno, CA

Asian Style Wonton
Makes 24

24 wonton wrappers
vegetable spray
5 ounces chicken, cooked, diced
$1/4$ cup mayonnaise
$1/2$ teaspoon Emeril's Asian seasoning
1" section ginger root, peeled, pressed
8 ounces water chestnuts, drained, chopped
$1/4$ cup carrot, peeled, grated
$1/4$ cup red bell pepper, diced
1 teaspoon fresh or dried parsley

Preheat oven to 350 degrees. Press wontons into small muffin pan allowing tops to stick up over edges. Spray with vegetable spray. Bake wonton shells 8

5

to 10 minutes. Add all remaining ingredients to bowl and combine thoroughly. Using 1 ounce scoop, place mixture into each of the wonton shells. Garnish as desired.

Jan Albano   Granite Bay High School, Granite Bay, CA

Bacon & Mushroom Bite-Sized Quiche

(Photo opposite page 32)

Makes 3 1/2 dozen

> pastry for double-crust pie (homemade or purchased)
> 8 slices bacon
> 1/4 pound fresh mushrooms, chopped
> 1 tablespoon butter
> 1/3 cup green onion, chopped
> 1 2/3 cups Swiss cheese, shredded
> 5 eggs
> 1 2/3 cups sour cream

Preheat oven to 375 degrees. On a lightly floured board, roll out pastry dough. Using a 3" cutter, cut out 42 circles; re-roll scraps as needed. Fit circles into bottoms and slightly up sides of lightly greased 2 1/2" muffin pans. Meanwhile fry bacon until crisp; drain; crumble or chop. Chop mushrooms, saute in butter until limp and liquid evaporates. Combine bacon, mushrooms, green onion and cheese. Divide filling equally among muffin cups. In large bowl, beat together eggs, add sour cream and stir until smooth. Spoon about 1 tablespoon into each muffin cup. Bake until puffed and light brown, 20 to 25 minutes. Cool in pans 5 minutes; lift out. Serve warm or let cool on wire racks. If made ahead, wrap cooled quiches airtight and refrigerate overnight. Reheat, uncovered, in a 350 degree oven for about 10 minutes.

National Pork Board   www.theotherwhitemeat.com

Banana Muffin Treat

Serves 4

> 4 English muffins, split
> butter
> 2 bananas, peeled, sliced
> 8 slices Swiss cheese
> 8 slices cooked bacon, cut in half

Toast muffin halves; butter and place on baking sheet. Arrange banana slices on muffins. Top with a slice of cheese. Criss-cross with 2 slices bacon (halves). Place under broiler and cook until cheese melts.

"Something different!"

Wendy Duncan   West Covina High School, West Covina, CA

Boboli Pesto Bites

Serves 4

1 (large) package Boboli Bread
4 to 6 ounces cream cheese
$1/4$ to $1/2$ cup Christopher Ranch Pesto
$1/4$ to $1/2$ cup sun dried tomatoes
$1/4$ cup pine nuts

Preheat oven to 450 degrees. Layer the Boboli bread with cream cheese, pesto, sun dried tomatoes and pine nuts. Place on foil-lined pizza pan or cookie sheet. Bake 8 to 10 minutes. Cut into pie wedges and serve hot. Note: Good with chicken pieces too!

"Karin Fitzhugh, three-sport Hall of Famer from Chico State, introduced me to a version of this recipe. She's now a teacher and coach at Central Valley"

Peggy Herndon　　　　**Central Valley High School, Shasta Lake City, CA**

Chili-Cheese Dip

Makes about 2 cups

1 pound Velveeta cheese, cut into cubes
1 (4 ounce) can chopped green chiles
1 teaspoon Worcestershire sauce
1 (15 ounce) can Hormel chili, with beans

Crockpot
RECIPE!

Mix all ingredients together in a crockpot. Heat until cheese is melted. Serve hot with corn chips.

"Quick and easy and tastes great. The flavor varies with the type of chili used and our family prefers Hormel. One of the great fix-it-and-forget-it recipes. Just put the temp low on the crockpot when it is melted."

Elizabeth Thornburg　　　　**Selma High School, Selma, CA**

Cool Avocado Dip

Makes about 1 $1/2$ cups

2 ripe avocados
2 tablespoons sweet onion, chopped
$1/2$ jalapeño (or to desired heat)
$1/4$ bunch cilantro ($1/3$ cup)
2 Roma tomatoes, cut into chunks
1 cucumber, seeded and cut into chunks
1 tablespoon fresh lime juice

Mash the ripe avocados with a fork in a bowl. Place remaining ingredients into a food processor and pulse until chopped fine. Add chopped ingredients to the avocado and mix well. Serve chilled with your favorite chips or southwest dish or on top of chicken or fish.

Sheri Crouse　　　　**Rhodes Junior High School, Mesa, AZ**

Grilled Mushrooms

Serves 4

12 (large) fresh mushrooms
2 tablespoons olive oil
2 cloves garlic, minced
1 tablespoon fresh oregano, minced or 1 teaspoon dried oregano
1 teaspoon salt
1/4 teaspoon pepper
lemon wedges

Prepare a hot fire in a grill or preheat broiler. Wipe mushrooms clean with a damp towel. Cut stem ends level with caps. In a small bowl, combine olive oil, garlic and oregano. Brush mushrooms with oil mixture. Season with salt and pepper. Place mushroom caps, stem side down, on oiled grill rack or in a broiler pan set 4" to 6" from heat. Grill or broil 3 to 5 minutes until well marked from grill. Turn over and cook 3 minutes longer, or until mushrooms are tender but still hold their shape. Serve with lemon wedges.

"A quick and easy appetizer that's quite tasty!"

Mary Coffman   Reed High School, Sparks, NV

Hot Chili Cheese Dip

Crockpot RECIPE!

Makes 6 cups

1 (medium) onion finely chopped
2 cloves garlic, minced
2 teaspoons vegetable oil
2 (15 ounce) cans chili, without beans
2 cups salsa
1 (2 to 3 ounce) package cream cheese, cubed
2 (2.25 ounce) cans ripe olives, sliced, drained
tortilla chips

Sauté onion and garlic in oil until tender. Transfer to a slow cooker. Stir in the chili, salsa, cream cheese and olives. Cover and cook on low for 4 hours or until heated through, stirring occasionally. Serve with tortilla chips.

Diana Lee   David A. Brown Middle School, Wildomar, CA

Meatballs in Raspberry Chipotle Sauce

Crockpot RECIPE!

Serves 10 - 12

meatballs, cooked
1 bottle raspberry chipotle sauce

Place cooked meatballs in crockpot and cover with raspberry chipotle sauce. Heat until meatballs are heated through, about 30 minutes on medium-high setting. Reduce heat to keep warm.

"So easy and good. Definitely a favorite with party guests!"

Susan Lefler   Ramona Junior High School, Chino, CA

Mexican Corn Salsa
Serves 8 - 10

1/4 cup vegetable oil
2 tablespoons red wine vinegar
1/4 teaspoon salt
1/8 teaspoon hot pepper sauce (or to taste)
1 (16 ounce) can black beans, drained, rinsed
1 (11 ounce) can Mexican style corn, drained
1 bunch green onions, diced
1 tomato, finely chopped
1 avocado, peeled, chopped

Mix all ingredients together. Refrigerate 3 hours or overnight.

"Super! A summer BBQ must have! Serve this with tortilla chips!"

Barbara Correia   Foothill High School, Pleasanton, CA

Mexican Style Shrimp Cocktail
Serves 6

1 (14 to 16 ounce) bag frozen shrimp, uncooked,
  peeled, deveined with no tail
4 cups of water
2 (large) tomatoes, diced
1 (small) cucumber diced
1 (small) red onion, finely diced
1/2 bunch cilantro, leaves only
1/4 fresh jalapeño chile, minced
2 avocados, medium diced
1 (small) bottle ketchup
juice of 3 squeezed lemons
1/2 teaspoon salt
1/4 teaspoon pepper
saltine crackers or tortilla chips, diced avocado

In medium saucepan, bring water to a boil. Add shrimp and cook 4 to 7 minutes or until shrimp begins to turn pink in color; drain in large colander, reserving 1 cup of the broth. Place broth in the freezer to chill. Place cooked shrimp on large plate and chill in the freezer for about 5 minutes. Take shrimp and broth out of the freezer and place in a large bowl. Add the tomatoes, red onion, cilantro and chile. Stir in the 1 cup reserved broth, ketchup, lemon juice, salt and pepper. Serve in small bowls, garnished with diced avocado and accompany with saltine crackers or tortilla chips.

"Excellent on a hot summer day! If you are on the Atkins diet, substitute regular ketchup with sugar-free ketchup found in health food stores."

Elvia Nieto   Alhambra High School, Alhambra, CA

Morning Fruit Shake

Serves 4

1 cup cranberry juice
2 (medium) bananas, sliced
2 (8 ounce) cartons raspberry yogurt
1 tablespoon confectioner's sugar, optional

In a blender, combine all ingredients; blend at medium speed until smooth. Serve immediately.

Diana Lee   David A. Brown Middle School, Wildomar, CA

Muffy's Microwave Caramel Corn

Serves 8

16 cups popcorn, popped
1 cup brown sugar
1/2 cup margarine
1/4 cup corn syrup
1/2 teaspoon salt
1 teaspoon vanilla
1/2 teaspoon baking soda

Place popcorn in large paper bag. In microwave bowl, combine brown sugar with margarine, corn syrup and salt. Microwave on high 1 to 2 minutes; stir. Boil 2 minutes, stirring after each minute. Add vanilla and baking soda; stir well. Pour over popcorn in paper bag. Roll down bag to close. Microwave bag 1 minute; shake bag. Repeat. Microwave bag 30 seconds more; shake bag. Repeat. Pour out coated popcorn onto counter or waxed paper to cool.

"Fast and easy snack. Once you start eating - you just can't stop!"

Julie Ericksen   Skyline High School, Salt Lake City, UT

Orange Julius Blender Beverage

Serves 4

1 (6 ounce) can frozen orange juice concentrate
1 cup milk
1 cup water
1/4 cup sugar
1/2 teaspoon vanilla
10 ice cubes or 1 cup crushed ice

Put all ingredients in blender, adding ice last. Process until smooth. Pour into glasses and enjoy!

"A great breakfast or snack smoothie. This has been a favorite of foods class students for many years. Add a banana or other fruit for a change."

Leigh Ann Diffenderfer   Newbury Park High School, Newbury Park, CA

Pizza Snacks
Serves 4

4 English Muffins
1 cup prepared pizza sauce
1 cup mozzarella cheese, shredded
Optional Toppings: Pepperoni or your choice of meat;
   sliced mushrooms; chopped onion; olives

Preheat broiler. Place English muffin halves, crust-side down, on broiler pan. At this point, muffins may be slightly toasted. Spread each muffin half with 2 tablespoons pizza sauce. Top with preferred toppings. Sprinkle each muffin half with 2 tablespoons cheese. Position broiler pan so the tops of the muffins are about 4 inches from the heat. Broil until cheese is bubbly, about 2 minutes. Remove and serve immediately.

"These are easy, fun and good. Students enjoy this in lab."

Liz Aschenbrenner   Sierra High School, Manteca, CA

Proscuitto, Apple & Brie Brushetta
Makes 16

1 baguette
$1/4$ cup garlic oil
4 ounces proscuitto
1 Granny Smith apple, sliced
4 $1/2$ ounces brie cheese

Slice baguette into 16 slices. Brush each slice with garlic oil and broil on a cookie sheet until toasted. Layer each slice with proscuitto, apple and brie. If desired, broil again until cheese is melted. Serve.

"This is so easy and a great last-minute appetizer!"

Leslie Corsini   Nicolas Junior High School, Fullerton, CA

Punch on the Go
Serves 15 - 20

1 orange
1 lemon
5 to 6 strawberries
1 gallon cranberry peach juice
1 liter ginger ale
1 (12 ounce) container lemonade concentrate
1 ice ring, with lemon, orange and strawberry slices

Two days ahead of serving, slice orange, lemon and strawberries and place in a ring mold or ice holder; fill half way up sides with water. Place in freezer. The next day, fill the mold to the top with water and return to freezer. (This allows you to arrange fruits in an interesting manner without random floating.) Before serving, unmold ice ring by running cold water over it until it falls out. Place remaining ingredients in a punch bowl and float ice ring on top.

"Very easy and very refreshing. If your punch bowl is large enough, you can also add loose ice cubes. Mint sprigs add a fresh feel and can also float with the ice ring."

Larkin Evans   Half Moon Bay High School, Half Moon Bay, CA

Raspberry Chipotle Brie Bites
Serves 6

Olive oil flavored nonstick cooking spray
1 baguette, thinly sliced (about 24 slices)
8 ounces brie, sliced
1 cup bottled raspberry chipotle sauce

Spray the baguette slices with nonstick cooking spray on both sides and broil until lightly browned. Place a slice of brie and a teaspoon of raspberry chipolte sauce on each baguette slice. Broil until cheese melts and serve hot.

"You can find bottled raspberry chipotle sauce with other bottled sauces in most grocery stores."

Tisha Ludeman   Brookhurst Junior High School, Anaheim, CA

Shrimp, Tomato & Cheese Quesadilla
Serves 4

8 ounces bay shrimp, cooked
$1/2$ cup fresh tomatoes, chopped
2 cups jack cheese, grated
4 tablespoons fresh cilantro, coarsely chopped
8 (8") flour tortillas
1 ripe avocado, peeled, thinly sliced
salt and pepper, to taste
4 tablespoons butter or oil, divided

Evenly divide shrimp, tomatoes, cheese and cilantro among 4 tortillas, leaving 1" border around edge. Arrange avocado on top. Season to taste with salt and pepper. Set the 4 remaining tortillas on top, pressing gently to secure. In a 9" skillet, heat 1 tablespoon butter or oil over medium heat. Place one quesadilla in the pan and cook until cheese melts and tortilla crisps to a golden brown. Carefully flip the quesadilla and repeat on the other side. Transfer to a cutting board and cover with foil. Let stand 2 minutes before cutting into wedges. Repeat with remaining quesadillas. Serve immediately.

"Crab meat or any meat filling can be substituted for the shrimp."

Kathie Baczynski   Mt. Carmel High School, Poway, CA

Spicy Orange Wings

Serves 6

(Photo opposite page 33)

2 tablespoons Lawry's Seasoned Salt
1 tablespoon Lawry's Seasoned Pepper
4 pounds chicken wings, tips removed (about 20 wings)
4 tablespoons margarine
1 (18 ounce) jar orange marmalade
$1/4$ teaspoon cayenne pepper

In a large ziploc bag, combine seasoned salt and pepper. Add chicken and toss to evenly coat. In large heavy skillet, heat margarine over medium heat. Add wings to skillet and cook 20 minutes, or until thoroughly cooked, turning frequently to brown on all sides. Transfer wings to platter and keep warm. Wipe out skillet with paper towels. Add marmalade and cayenne to skillet. Bring to a boil and cook over medium heat for about 3 minutes. Return cooked wings to skillet and heat through, about 5 minutes, tossing to coat evenly with glaze. Cool 7 to 10 minutes before serving. Note: For spicier wings, increase cayenne pepper to $1/2$ teaspoon.

Lawry's Foods, Inc.   www.lawrys.com

Strawberry Punch

Makes 1 gallon

1 (2 liter) bottle of 7-Up soda
2 cups strawberry daiquiri mix
Water
1 bag frozen strawberries or other type of berries

Pour 7-Up soda and strawberry daiquiri mix into a large punch bowl. Add water to your desired taste. Stir in frozen fruit and serve. Add additional frozen fruit as needed, to keep punch cold.

"Everyone loves this simple punch.
The frozen fruit ice is a nice touch and adds flavor."

Christina Sargent   Delano High School, Delano, CA

Strawberry Swirl

Serves 2-3

$1/2$ pint strawberries (1 cup)
1 cup lowfat milk (1% or 2%)
1 tablespoon sugar
$1/2$ teaspoon vanilla
2 ice cubes, crushed

Clean berries. Combine all ingredients in a blender, whirring at high speed until pureed and fluffy. Pour into glasses and serve.

"Great for a quick pick-me-up in the afternoon."

Dotti Jones   Etiwanda High School, Etiwanda, CA

Stuffed Mushrooms

Serves 8 - 10

1 pound mushrooms
1 pound bacon, diced, cooked and drained
3 green onions, diced
2 (8 ounce) packages cream cheese, softened

Preheat oven to 350 degrees. Remove stems from mushrooms and chop finely in food processor. Mix with remaining ingredients. Stuff mushroom caps with mixture and bake in a 9"x 13" pan for 20 minutes or until heated through.

"These are always a hit at parties!"

Jane Reed   Dublin High School, Dublin, CA

Sweet Popcorn Snack Mix

Makes 2 1/2 quarts

8 cups popped corn
2 tablespoons cinnamon-sugar
1 tablespoon baking cocoa
1 cup bear-shaped graham snacks
1 cup thin pretzel sticks, broken
1 cup plain M&M candies

Place popcorn in large bowl. Combine cinnamon sugar and cocoa. Toss with popcorn. Stir in remaining ingredients. Store in airtight container.

"I found this in a fast and easy cookbook.
It is great for the preschool we have at school every Friday."

Robin Ali   Nevada Union High School, Grass Valley, CA

Swiss and Bacon Dip

Makes about 2 cups

8 slices bacon, chopped
8 ounces cream cheese, softened
1/2 cup mayonnaise
2 rounded teaspoons prepared Dijon mustard
1 1/2 cups Swiss cheese, shredded
3 scallions, chopped
2 rounded teaspoons horseradish (optional)
1/2 cup smoked almonds, coarsely chopped
Baby carrots, celery, flat breads or baguettes

Preheat oven to 400 degrees. Brown bacon over medium heat. Drain on paper towels. Combine cream cheese, mayonnaise, Dijon mustard, Swiss cheese, scallions and horseradish, if using, with cooked bacon. Place mixture in small baking dish and bake until golden & bubbly at edges. Remove from oven and sprinkle with chopped almonds. Place dip on platter and surround with breads and vegetables.

"I saw this on Rachel Ray's 30 Minutes or Less *show. Everyone who tries this wants the recipe."*

Penny Childers   Ramona High School, Ramona, California

Toffee Apple Dip

Makes approx. 2 cups

1 (8 ounce) package cream cheese, softened
$1/2$ cup powdered sugar
$3/4$ cup brown sugar
1 teaspoon vanilla extract
$3/4$ cup Heath toffee chips (found in baking aisle)
sliced apples, soaked in pineapple or lemon juice
    to prevent browning (best with tart apples, such as
    Granny Smith or Pippin)

Whip cream cheese with mixer and add sugars and vanilla; mix thoroughly. Fold in toffee chips right before serving to prevent chips from becoming soggy. Serve with drained apple slices.

"Enjoy! This recipe comes from my sister-in-law, Tami Engel. Delicious!"

Adriana Molinaro   Granite Hills High School, El Cajon, CA

Breads and Bakery Items

Almost Red Lobster Drop Biscuits

Makes 1 dozen

2 cups all purpose flour
5 teaspoons baking powder
$1/2$ teaspoon salt
2 teaspoons sugar
$1/4$ teaspoon garlic powder
1 tablespoon dried parsley, chives, or onion flakes
$1/8$ teaspoon cayenne pepper
1 cube butter, melted, cooled to room temperature
1 cup milk
1 $1/2$ cups cheddar cheese, grated

Preheat oven to 375 degrees. Blend flour, baking powder, salt, sugar, garlic powder, dried herb, and cayenne pepper. Add butter and milk to dry ingredients. Stir in cheese and mix until just combined. Drop by spoonfuls onto parchment covered baking sheet. Bake 16 minutes.

"Great served with an omelet, soup, salad, enchiladas or just to snack!!!"

Priscilla Burns   Pleasant Valley High School, Chico, CA

Audra's Cheese Bread

Serves 4 - 6

nonstick cooking spray
1 (16.3 ounce) can Grands Pillsbury biscuits
1 cup cheddar cheese, grated

Preheat oven to 350 degrees. Spray loaf pan with nonstick cooking spray. Place roll of biscuits into loaf pan. Cut $3/4$" deep through center of all biscuits. Fan biscuits out to sides of loaf pan. Sprinkle cheese down center of cut biscuits. Bake 30 to 40 minutes until dough is thoroughly baked and golden brown. Serve warm.

"Along with teaching, my daughter wears the hat of a Pampered Chef consultant. This is her favorite simple, attractive and delicious recipe to share at parties."

Gerry Henderson   Temple City High School, Temple City, CA

Baked French Toast

Serves 4

1 baguette French bread, cut into 1" thick slices
6 (large) eggs
1 $1/2$ cups milk
1 cup half & half
1 teaspoon vanilla
$1/4$ teaspoon cinnamon
$1/4$ teaspoon nutmeg
$1/4$ cup butter or margarine, softened
$1/2$ cup light brown sugar
$1/2$ cup walnuts, chopped
1 tablespoon light corn syrup

Night before: Butter a 9" square baking dish. Arrange bread slices, overlapping to fill pan completely. Combine eggs, milk, half & half, vanilla, cinnamon and nutmeg. Mix well, then pour over bread slices. Cover and refrigerate overnight. *Next day:* Preheat oven to 350 degrees. Combine butter with brown sugar, walnuts and corn syrup. Mix well, then spread evenly over soaked bread in pan. Bake 40 minutes or until done.

"Make this ahead the night before - then just bake in the morning."

Millie Deeton   Ruben S. Ayala High School, Chino Hills, CA

Beignets (French Doughnuts)

Serves 6 - 8

2 to 3 cups cooking oil
1 loaf Bridgford dough, thawed
flour, for cutting board
powdered sugar

Heat oil over medium-high heat in deep saucepan. Cut thawed dough into $1/2$" thick slices. Flour a cutting board and flatten dough slices. Cut each slice into thirds. Deep fry, turning, until all are golden brown. Drain on paper towels. Roll in powdered sugar.

Doris Barela-Fossen   Sierra Vista Junior High School, Canyon Country, CA

Cheddar Cheese Biscuits

Makes 8

1 cup biscuit mix
$1/2$ cup sharp cheddar cheese, grated
$1/4$ to $1/3$ cup milk

Preheat oven to 450 degrees. Combine biscuit mix and cheese; add milk, stirring just until dry ingredients are moistened. (Dough will be very soft.) Turn dough out onto a floured surface and knead lightly 3 to 4 times. Roll dough to $1/2$" thickness; cut into rounds with a biscuit cutter. Place on lightly greased baking sheet. Bake 10 minutes. Serve immediately.

Judy Dobkins   Redlands High School, Redlands, CA

Creme Brulée French Toast

Serves 6

1 stick ($1/2$ cup) unsalted butter
1 cup brown sugar, packed
2 tablespoons corn syrup
1 loaf country-style bread, crusts removed
5 (large) eggs
1 $1/2$ cups half & half
1 teaspoon vanilla
$1/4$ teaspoon salt
Optional: 1 teaspoon Grand Marnier

In a small heavy saucepan, melt butter with brown sugar and corn syrup over moderate heat, stirring until smooth and pour into a 9" x 13" baking dish. Arrange bread slices in one layer in baking dish, squeezing them slightly to fit. In a bowl, whisk together the eggs, half & half, vanilla, Grand Marnier and salt until combined well and pour evenly over bread. Chill bread mixture, covered, overnight. Preheat oven to 350 degrees. Bake bread mixture, uncovered, in middle of oven until puffed and edges are pale golden, about 35 to 40 minutes. Serve immediately.

"This is a great recipe for an easy, quick and delicious
brunch or breakfast dish for company."

Betty Wells   Bidwell Junior High School, Chico, CA.

DutchBabies and Strawberries

Serves 4

$1/2$ cup margarine or butter
1 $1/4$ cups milk
$3/4$ cup flour
5 to 6 eggs
1 teaspoon vanilla
fresh strawberries
Cool Whip

Preheat oven to 350 degrees. Preheat a skillet and melt butter or margarine. While that melts, blend milk with flour; add eggs and vanilla. Pour into skillet, then transfer to oven and bake 25 to 30 minutes. While it cooks, it will rise, then fall as it cools. Top with fresh strawberries and powdered sugar.

"These are great for brunch or dessert in a hurry!"

Doris Richmond   Tulare Western High School, Tulare, CA

Easy Pancakes from Scratch
Serves 4 - 6

1 1/3 cups all-purpose flour
2 tablespoons sugar
1 tablespoon baking powder
1/2 teaspoon salt
1 egg
1 cup milk
3 tablespoons vegetable oil

In a small bowl, combine flour, sugar, baking powder and salt. Combine egg, milk and oil; stir into dry ingredients just until combined. Pour batter by 1/3 cupfuls onto lightly greased hot griddle or skillet. Turn when bubbles form on top of pancake; cook until second side is golden brown.

"I make these ahead of time and store them in the freezer. When my own children want pancakes for breakfast, they can just pop them in the toaster oven to heat."

Astrid Curfman   Newcomb Academy, Long Beach, CA

Moist Cornbread Muffins
Makes 12

2 eggs
1/4 cup granulated sugar
1 cup all-purpose flour
2/3 cup yellow cornmeal
2 teaspoons baking powder
1/2 teaspoon baking soda
1/2 teaspoon salt
1 cup plain yogurt
1/4 cup butter or margarine, melted

Preheat oven to 400 degrees. Beat together eggs and sugar. In another bowl, combine flour, cornmeal, baking powder, baking soda and salt. Add flour mixture, yogurt and melted butter to egg mixture. Stir just until evenly moistened. Spoon batter evenly into 12 paper-lined or well-greased muffin tins. Bake 18 to 20 minutes, until tops are lightly browned and centers are firm when gently touched.

Marguerite Smith   Murrieta Valley High School, Murrieta, CA

Oven Baked Chocolate Chip Pancakes

Serves 6

2 cups Bisquick
1 $1/2$ cups milk
1 egg
2 tablespoons cooking oil
$1/4$ cup miniature chocolate chips
butter, syrup

Preheat oven to 425 degrees. In medium mixing bowl, stir together Bisquick, milk, eggs and oil. Batter will be lumpy. Stir in chocolate chips. Pour batter into 15-$1/2$" x 10-$1/2$" x 1" baking pan. Bake about 10 minutes or until well done. Cut into squares. Serve with butter and syrup, if desired.

"This is so much faster than cooking a few pancakes at a time
and everyone gets to eat at the same time!"

Paula Skrifvars   Brea Junior High School, Brea, CA

Raised Whole Wheat Waffles

Makes 8

1 package (2 $1/4$ teaspoons) active dry yeast
$1/2$ cup warm water
2 cups warm milk
1 stick (or less) butter, melted
1 teaspoon sugar
1 teaspoon salt
1 cup all-purpose flour
1 cup whole wheat flour
2 eggs
$1/4$ teaspoon baking soda

Sprinkle yeast over warm water in a large mixing bowl and let stand 5 minutes. Add milk, butter, sugar, salt and both flours. Beat until smooth. Cover and let stand overnight in refrigerator. When ready to cook, beat in eggs and baking soda. The batter will be thin. Bake in a hot waffle iron, using $1/2$ to $3/4$ cup batter for each waffle.

"The batter will keep several days in the refrigerator
(be sure to keep it in a large container because the yeast will continue to work).
It is great to have on hand for company or a special family breakfast."

Linda Vincent   Turlock High School, Turlock, CA

Refrigerator Pumpkin Bran Muffins
Makes several dozen

2 cups whole bran cereal
1 $1/2$ cups buttermilk
1 cup canned pumpkin
$1/2$ cup vegetable oil
2 teaspoons orange zest, grated
2 eggs
2 $1/2$ cups flour
1 $1/2$ cups sugar
1 teaspoon baking powder
1 teaspoon baking soda
1 teaspoon cinnamon
$1/2$ teaspoon salt
$1/4$ teaspoon each cloves and allspice
1 cup raisins or dried cranberries
$1/4$ cup nuts, chopped

In a large bowl, combine cereal and buttermilk. Let stand 5 minutes to soften cereal. Add pumpkin, oil, orange zest and eggs; blend well. Stir in flour, sugar, and spices. Fold in dried fruit and nuts. Batter may be baked immediately or stored up to two weeks in the refrigerator in a tightly covered container. To bake in conventional oven, preheat to 400 degrees. Grease or line muffin pans with muffin papers. Fill each well $3/4$ full. Sprinkle each muffin with sugar. Bake 18 to 22 minutes.

"This is wonderful to have on hand, especially during the busy holidays. The muffins can also be baked in the microwave. Just line custard cups or a microwave-safe muffin pan with muffin papers. Two muffins bake in 2 minutes on high power; 4 muffins bake in 2 to 3 minutes and 6 muffins in 3 to 3 $1/2$ minutes."

Laura de la Motte   Turlock High School, Turlock, CA

Scones
Serves 4

1 $1/4$ cups flour
1 $1/2$ teaspoons baking powder
$1/4$ teaspoon salt
$1/4$ cup unsalted butter, cold
3 tablespoons sugar
$1/2$ cup whipping cream

Preheat oven to 425 degrees. In a medium bowl, combine flour, baking powder and salt. Cut cold butter into pieces; then using a pastry blender, cut butter into the flour mixture until particles are about the size of small peas. Sprinkle on sugar and toss with a fork to blend. Add cream, stirring mixture with fork until ingredients begin to hold together. Gather into ball, place on lightly floured surface and knead gently 10 to 12 times. Pat dough into 6" circle. Cut into 6 to 8 wedges. Place on ungreased baking sheet, slightly apart so sides will crisp. Bake 12 to 15 minutes, until tops are light golden brown. Remove scones from oven and transfer to kitchen towel placed over wire rack. Cover scones loosely with remainder of towel and cool 30 minutes before serving.

"This L.A. Times recipe is great. I use this in class and the students love it."

Reiko Ikkanda   South Pasadena Middle School, South Pasadena, CA

Sourdough Crescent Rolls
Makes 1 dozen

> 1 cup biscuit mix
> 1 tablespoon sugar
> $1/_2$ teaspoon baking soda
> 2 tablespoons butter
> $1/_2$ cup sourdough starter

Preheat oven to 400 degrees. Combine biscuit mix, sugar, and baking soda. Cut in butter until no large particles remain. Add starter and stir just to blended. (If too dry, add 1 tablespoon milk.) Knead one minute. Divide dough in half and roll into 9" circles. Brush with melted butter and cut each into 6 wedges. Roll each piece from large end to small end making crescents. Place on baking sheet and bake 12 minutes.

"This was given to me by my friend, Laurie Frazier, from Ceres High School."

Lori Konschak   Ceres High School, Ceres, CA

Sourdough Starter
Makes about 3 cups

> 2 cups flour
> 2 cups warm water
> 1 tablespoon yeast

Combine flour, water, and yeast in a glass or plastic container. Let rise in a warm place overnight. (This can be kept several days at room temperature or refrigerated for a longer period of time.) To replenish, add equal parts of flour and warm water and set at room temperature for several hours.

"I like this overnight starter because I can make sourdough pizza the next day."

Lori Konschak   Ceres High School, Ceres, CA

Streusel Blueberry Coffee Cake
Serves 9

2 cups all-purpose flour
$3/4$ cup sugar
$2/3$ cup milk
$1/4$ cup butter, softened
1 egg
2 teaspoons baking powder
$1/2$ teaspoon salt
$1/4$ teaspoon ground nutmeg
1 cup fresh or frozen blueberries
Topping:
$1/2$ cup sugar
$1/3$ cup all-purpose flour
$1/2$ teaspoon cinnamon
$1/2$ teaspoon nutmeg
$1/4$ cup cold butter

Preheat oven to 375 degrees. Combine all cake ingredients, except blueberries, in large mixer bowl. Beat at low speed, scraping bowl often, until well mixed, 1 to 2 minutes. Gently stir in blueberries by hand. Spread batter into 8" square baking pan sprayed with cooking spray. Stir together all streusel ingredients except butter in small bowl; cut in butter until mixture resembles coarse crumbs. Sprinkle mixture over batter. Bake 40 to 45 minutes or until toothpick inserted in center comes out clean. Serve warm.

"I use fresh blueberries in season and frozen the rest of the year.
This is a sfavorite at our house."

Julie Shelburne   Tulare Union High School, Tulare, CA

Surprise Scones
Makes 6

1 egg
1 tablespoon water
2 $1/2$ cups flour
$1/4$ cup sugar
2 teaspoons baking powder
$1/2$ teaspoon salt
$1/4$ cup margarine
$7/8$ cup milk
$1/2$ cup desired ingredient: Chocolate chips; dried or fresh fruit,
   diced; chopped nuts

Preheat oven to 400 degrees. Lightly grease a baking sheet. Beat egg and water; set aside. Combine flour, sugar, baking powder and salt. Cut in margarine. Stir in milk and egg mixture until moist. Fold in $1/2$ cup desired ingredient. Drop into 6 blobs onto baking sheet. Bake 20 to 25 minutes.

"Creative and delicious, especially with milk or tea."

Dale Sheehan   Santana High School, Santee, CA

Wheat Bread
Makes 1 loaf

1 package yeast
1 $1/2$ cups bread flour
1 $1/2$ cups wheat four
$1/2$ teaspoon salt
2 (medium) ripe bananas, sliced
$1/4$ cup warm water
$1/4$ cup honey
1 egg
$1/4$ cup oil
$1/2$ teaspoon vanilla
1 teaspoon poppy seeds

Using an electric breadmaker: Add ingredients in order above to breadmaker. Turn the machine "on" and cook according to breadmaker's instructions, about 1 $1/2$ hours. Note: Put overripe bananas, peel and all, in a ziploc bag and freeze until you're ready to make bread. Thaw in microwave, peel and use in this yummy recipe.

"You'll never buy store-bought bread again!"

Debi Spencer   Colton High School, Colton, CA

www.race (Whole Wheat Waffles - Fast)
Serves 6

6 eggs
2 cups milk
2 teaspoons lemon juice or 2 tablespoons orange juice
1 teaspoon baking soda
$1/4$ teaspoon salt
$1/4$ cup oil
2 $1/2$ cups whole wheat flour
nonstick cookong spray

Stir egg with a fork to break up yolks. Add milk and lemon or orange juice to sour the milk. Add baking soda, salt, oil and flour. Mix well. Spray waffle iron with nonstick cooking spray as soon as iron is heated. Watch iron for reduction of steam to signal waffle readiness (often before iron light says it's ready). Gently peek to see if waffle is browned. Spray iron every other waffle.

"This is so fast to make I race my waffle iron! Plugging in the iron starts the race. I can usually have the batter mixed before the waffle iron light goes out to let me know it's heated up and ready to bake the waffles!"

Cyndi Matthews   Etiwanda High School, Etiwanda, CA

Soups Stews *and* Chili

Best Potato Soup Ever

Serves 4 - 6

    diced potatoes
    diced celery
    diced carrots
    diced onion
    cream cheese

Barely cover vegetables with water and bring to a boil. Cook until vegetables are soft. Drop in cream cheese. Melt and enjoy. Note: Vary the amounts of ingredients to suit your serving needs.

"Quick, delicious and heart healthy with reduced fat cream cheese."

Dr. Terry Kluever   **Coronado High School, Henderson, NV**

Cheddar Cheese Potato Soup

Serves 6

    2 tablespoons oil
    1 onion, chopped
    2 tablespoons butter
    $1/4$ cup flour
    1 teaspoon salt
    $1/2$ teaspoon pepper
    6 cups chicken broth*
    4 cups potatoes, peeled, diced
    2 cups corn or broccoli (optional)
    1 cup half & half
    $1/2$ cup cheddar cheese, shredded

In a large stockpot over medium heat, sauté onions in oil until translucent, about 10 minutes. Add butter. Stir in flour, salt and pepper and cook 3 minutes. Add the chicken stock and potatoes; (if using broccoli, add now), bring to a boil, and simmer, uncovered, 15 minutes until potatoes are tender. (If using corn, add to soup and cook 10 minutes). Add half & half and cheese. Cook 5 minutes more until cheese is melted. Season to taste with salt and pepper. Serve hot. *To make broth:* Add 6 teaspoons chicken base to 6 cups warm water; stir to dissolve.

Pat Freshour   Foothill High School, Redding, CA

Cheddar Cheese Soup

Makes 4 cups

$1/2$ onion, chopped
1 rib of celery, sliced
2 tablespoons margarine
2 tablespoons all-purpose flour
$1/4$ teaspoon pepper
$1/4$ teaspoon dry mustard
1 cup milk
$1/4$ cup hot water
1 cup chicken stock or 1 cup water and 1 teaspoon chicken base
2 cups shredded cheddar cheese (8 ounces)

Cover and cook onion and celery in margarine in 2-quart sauce pan over medium heat for about 5 minutes or until onion is tender. Stir in flour, pepper and mustard. Add milk, water and chicken stock. Heat to boiling over medium heat, stirring constantly. Boil and stir one minute. Remove from heat, stir in cheese. You can add cooked broccoli or other vegetables to this for a vegetable cheese soup.

"My students love this soup and it is very quick and easy."

Shauna Young   Jordan High School, Sandy, UT

Cheesy Ham Chowder

Serves 8

$1/4$ cup butter or margarine
$3/4$ cup onion, chopped
2 cloves garlic, minced
$1/4$ cup flour
4 cups chicken broth
6 (large) potatoes, cubed
1 (16 ounce) bag frozen sweet yellow corn
3 to 4 cups cooked ham, chopped
1 (12 ounce) can evaporated milk
8 to 12 ounces Colby cheese, shredded
salt and pepper to taste

Melt the butter in a Dutch oven over medium heat. Add onion and garlic and sauté until tender and the onions are translucent. Incorporate flour with a wire whisk until well blended. Cook for 45 to 60 seconds. Slowly add chicken broth to mixture and whisk until there are no lumps. Add chopped potatoes and bring to a boil. Simmer for 15 to 20 minutes until the potatoes are tender. Add corn and ham. Simmer 10 to 15 minutes until the chowder is hot all the way through. Add milk, cheese, and salt and pepper. Stir until the cheese is melted.

"This is a great one pan chowder. Kids really like this one!!"

Nicole Rehmann   La Mesa Junior High School, Santa Clarita, CA

Chicken Enchilada Soup

Serves 8

 1 tablespoon vegetable oil
 3 chicken breast fillets, about 1 pound
 $1/3$ cup onion, diced
 1 clove garlic, pressed
 4 cups chicken broth
 1 cup masa harina
   (found in the Hispanic section–looks like a bag of flour)
 3 cups water
 1 cup canned enchilada sauce
 16 ounces Velveeta cheese, cubed
 1 teaspoon salt
 1 teaspoon chili powder
 $1/2$ teaspoon cumin
 Optional: Shredded jalapeño jack cheese;
   crumbled tortilla chips; pico de gallo

Heat oil in large pot over medium heat. Add chicken breasts and brown 4 to 5 minutes per side. Remove chicken and set aside. Add onions and garlic to pot and sauté over medium heat about 2 minutes or until onions become translucent. Add chicken broth. Combine masa harina with 2 cups water in a medium bowl and whisk until blended. Add masa mixture to pot with onions, garlic and broth. Add remaining 1 cup water, enchilada sauce, cheese and spices to pot and bring to a boil. Shred chicken into small bite-size pieces and add to pot. Reduce heat and simmer 30 to 40 minutes or until thick. Serve in bowls garnished with shredded jalapeño jack cheese, crumbled tortilla chips and pico de gallo, if desired.

"I make this recipe with my students and they really like it!"

Jill Enright   Granite Hills High School, El Cajon, CA

Chicken Noodle Soup

Serves 6

6 cups chicken stock*
1 boneless, skinless chicken breast
1 yellow onion, finely diced
2 carrots, peeled, halved lengthwise and thinly sliced
2 celery stalks, thinly sliced
2 ounces egg noodles
3 tablespoons fresh parsley
salt and pepper to taste

In a large stockpot over medium heat, bring stock to a simmer. Add the chicken breast and simmer just until tender and no trace of pink remains, about 8 to 10 minutes. Remove from heat and let chicken cool. Transfer chicken to cutting board and cut into cubes. Return stock to a simmer over medium heat and add onion, carrots and celery. Simmer until vegetables are slightly softened, about 10 minutes, skimming away any foam that rises to surface of stock. Add cooked chicken, egg noodles, parsley, salt and pepper. Simmer until noodles are tender, about 3 minutes. *To make chicken broth:* Add 6 teaspoons chicken base to 6 cups warm water; stir to dissolve.

Pat Freshour   Foothill High School, Redding, CA

Chicken Noodle Soup with Zucchini & Tomatos

Serves 6

2 tablespoons extra virgin olive oil
1 (large) onion, chopped
8 cups good quality chicken broth
3 cloves garlic, minced
$1/2$ teaspoon dried thyme
$1/4$ teaspoon pepper
2 (large) carrots, thinly sliced
$1/2$ cup celery, chopped
5 ounces dried wide egg noodles
3 cups cooked chicken, shredded
1 (small) zucchini, chopped
1 (medium) tomato, peeled, seeded and chopped
2 tablespoons parsley

Heat oil in a 5 to 6 quart pan over medium high heat. Add onion, cooking and stirring until onion is soft. Add broth, garlic, thyme and pepper; bring to a boil. Stir in carrots, celery, and noodles. Reduce heat, cover and boil gently just until carrots are barely tender to the bite, about 10 minutes. Stir in chicken, zucchini, and tomato; heat until steaming. Garnish with parsley.

"Home made soup in less than $1/2$ hour! Delicious too! Use canned chicken to save time, or stir-fry 1 pound chicken tenders, diced and add to the broth

along with the noodles. I vary the veggies to what I happen to have on hand. Frozen green beans are good, too."

Myrna Swearingen   Corona High School, Corona, CA

Chicken Parmigiana
Serves 4

$^1/_2$ cup seasoned bread crumbs
2 tablespoons Parmesan cheese, grated
4 tablespoons butter, melted
4 boneless skinless chicken breasts
juice of 1 lemon

Preheat oven to 375 degrees. Combine seasoned bread crumbs with Parmesan cheese. Melt butter in microwave oven. Dip chicken pieces in butter first, then coat both sides with bread crumbs. Place on foil-lined baking sheet. Squeeze fresh lemon on chicken breasts and bake 30 minutes.

"Make sure to line the pan with foil–no pan to wash! Fast and easy!"

Anne Silveira   Shasta High School, Redding, CA

Chicken Taco Stew
Serves 6

5 or 6 boneless chicken breasts
1 (medium) onion, chopped
1 (15 ounce) can corn, undrained
1 (28 ounce) can diced tomatoes, undrained
1 can diced green chiles
1 (15 ounce) can pinto beans, undrained
$^1/_4$ cup taco seasoning
1 cup water
salt and pepper, to taste
1 package Fritos chips
1 $^1/_2$ cups Monterey jack cheese, grated

Microwave the chicken until done. Shred the chicken into small pieces. In a crockpot, add all ingredients, except cheese and Fritos, and cook for several hours to blend the flavors. Top with cheese and serve with the chips.

Mary Mondientz   Buchanan High School, Clovis, CA

Chicken Tortilla Soup
Serves 4 - 5

1 tablespoon oil
$1/2$ cup onion, chopped
2 (large) cloves garlic, minced
1 jalapeño, minced
$1/2$ teaspoon cumin
1 (15 ounce) can crushed tomatoes
5 cups chicken broth
1 cup chicken, cooked, chopped
3 to 4 corn tortillas, cut into 1 $1/2$" strips
Garnish: Shredded cheese, chopped avocado, chopped cilantro

Heat oil. Sauté onion, garlic, jalapeño and cumin for 4 minutes. Add tomatoes and broth and bring to a boil. Cover and simmer 20 minutes. Transfer to a food processor and blend until smooth. Return to pot and add chicken. Simmer 20 minutes. Add tortillas the last 10 minutes. Serve with garnishes.

"This is an easy recipe to prepare at school. If the students don't like jalapeños, you can substitute canned green chiles. The students love this recipe."

Diane Castro   Temecula Valley High School, Temecula, CA

Chile Chicken
Serves 4 - 6

8 ounces medium noodles, uncooked
$1/4$ cup onion, chopped
1 tablespoon margarine
2 cups chicken, cooked, diced
salt and pepper, to taste
1 can cream of mushroom soup
1 tablespoon pimiento, chopped
1 tablespoon green chile, finely chopped
1 teaspoon Italian seasoning
1 $1/2$ cups sharp cheddar cheese, shredded
1 teaspoon paprika

Preheat oven to 350 degrees. Cook noodles as directed; drain. In large skillet, cook and stir onion in margarine until tender. Add chopped cooked chicken, season with salt and pepper to taste. In small saucepan over low heat, heat soup with pimiento, chile and Italian seasoning. In a greased casserole dish, layer half of the noodles and half of the chicken. Top with half of the soup mixture and half of the cheese. Repeat layers, ending with cheese on top. Sprinkle paprika on top and bake, uncovered, about 30 minutes.

Alice Claiborne   Fairfield High School, Fairfield, CA

Chili Mac

Serves 4

1 pound ground beef
1 teaspoon garlic powder
1 can pork 'n beans
1 (8 ounce) can tomato sauce
1 $1/2$ cups water
$1/2$ pound rotelli pasta
1 teaspoon chili powder
$1/2$ teaspoon salt

Brown beef in large skillet, seasoning with garlic powder; drain well. Add pork 'n beans, tomato sauce and water. Bring to a boil. Stir in pasta, chili powder and salt. Cover with lid and reduce heat to low. Simmer 7 to 10 minutes or until pasta is cooked.

DeLisa Davis   **Sutter High School, Sutter, CA**

Chili Soup

Serves 4 - 6

3 (15 ounce) cans Hormel Chili, Turkey, No Beans
32 ounces chicken broth
1 (16 ounce) package frozen stir-fry vegetables
1 (14 ounce) package frozen pepper strips
1 (8 ounces) container organic baked tofu, savory or Thai flavor

Cut tofu into small cubes. Stir all ingredients together in a large pot. Stir occasionally over medium heat until hot. Note: Substitute your favorite frozen vegetables; omit tofu, if desired.

Becky Oppen   **Dana Hills High School, Dana Point, CA**

Creamy Tortilla Soup

Serves 6 - 8

2 cans cream of chicken soup
1 can milk
1 can chicken broth
2 cups cooked chicken, diced (optional)
$1/2$ cup salsa
$1/4$ cup green onions, chopped
$1/4$ cup diced green chiles
2 tablespoons taco seasoning
1 teaspoon ground cumin
tortilla chips, grated cheese, sour cream, guacamole

Crockpot RECIPE!

Whisk soup together with milk and broth. Stir in remaining ingredients and heat through, stirring often. Adjust seasoning to taste. Serve with crumbled tortilla chips, grated cheese, a dollop of sour cream and guacamole, as desired. Note: For thicker soup, use less broth or milk. This soup is good simmered in the crockpot on low heat.

"Here's a recipe the teachers discussed that I made recently. My family loved it. I think you'll like it too, Quick to fix and tastes good on a cold evening."

Lois Nielsen   West Jordan High School, West Jordan, UT

Double Quick Chili
Serves 4

2 (10.5 ounce) cans beans & bacon soup
2 (10.5 ounce) cans tomato soup
1 (10.5 ounce) can chili con carne, no beans
1 $1/4$ cups water

In saucepan, combine soups, chili and water. Simmer, uncovered for 10 minutes.

Deanna Lee   Marina High School, Huntington Beach, CA

Easy Clam Chowder
Serves 6

1 cup butter
1 $1/2$ cups celery, chopped
1 $1/2$ cups onion, chopped
1 $1/2$ cups green bell pepper, chopped
$1/4$ cup flour
5 cups hot milk
3 (6.5 ounce) clams and juice
2 cups potatoes, cooked, cubed
$1/2$ teaspoon thyme
salt and pepper, to taste

Heat butter in saucepan and sauté celery, onion and bell pepper until soft. Add flour and mix until smooth. Stir in hot milk, clams and juice. Cook 10 minutes. Add potatoes, thyme, salt and pepper. Mix and simmer over low heat for a few minutes until heated through.

"This takes about 40 minutes total to prepare! Goes great with warm French bread."

Lafonne Mize   Lemoore High School, Lemoore, CA

Bacon & Mushroom Bite-Sized Quiche

Makes 3 ¹/₂ dozen

pastry for double-crust pie (homemade or purchased)
8 slices bacon
¹/₄ pound fresh mushrooms, chopped
1 tablespoon butter
¹/₃ cup green onion, chopped
1 ²/₃ cups Swiss cheese, shredded
5 eggs
1 ²/₃ cups sour cream

Preheat oven to 375 degrees. On a lightly floured board, roll out pastry dough. Using a 3" cutter, cut out 42 circles; re-roll scraps as needed. Fit circles into bottoms and slightly up sides of lightly greased 2 ¹/₂" muffin pans. Meanwhile fry bacon until crisp; drain; crumble or chop. Chop mushrooms, saute in butter until limp and liquid evaporates. Combine bacon, mushrooms, green onion and cheese. Divide filling equally among muffin cups. In large bowl, beat together eggs, add sour cream and stir until smooth. Spoon about 1 tablespoon into each muffin cup. Bake until puffed and light brown, 20 to 25 minutes. Cool in pans 5 minutes; lift out. Serve warm or let cool on wire racks. If made ahead, wrap cooled quiches airtight and refrigerate overnight. Reheat, uncovered, in a 350 degree oven for about 10 minutes.

Spicy Orange Wings

Serves 6

    2 tablespoons Lawry's Seasoned Salt
    1 tablespoon Lawry's Seasoned Pepper
    4 pounds chicken wings, tips removed (about 20 wings)
    4 tablespoons margarine
    1 (18 ounce) jar orange marmalade
    $1/_4$ teaspoon cayenne pepper

In a large ziploc bag, combine seasoned salt and pepper. Add chicken and toss to evenly coat. In large heavy skillet, heat margarine over medium heat. Add wings to skillet and cook 20 minutes, or until thoroughly cooked, turning frequently to brown on all sides. Transfer wings to platter and keep warm. Wipe out skillet with paper towels. Add marmalade and cayenne to skillet. Bring to a boil and cook over medium heat for about 3 minutes. Return cooked wings to skillet and heat through, about 5 minutes, tossing to coat evenly with glaze. Cool 7 to 10 minutes before serving. Note: For spicier wings, increase cayenne pepper to $1/_4$ teaspoon.

Lawry's Foods, Inc.   www.lawrys.com

Fast Country Chicken Noodle Soup

Serves 4 - 5

48 ounces chicken broth
$1/4$ cup carrot, chopped
$1/4$ cup celery, chopped
1 tablespoon onion, finely chopped
1 tablespoon fresh parsley or 1 teaspoon dried parsley
$1/8$ teaspoon poultry seasoning
$1/8$ teaspoon crushed thyme
1 cup dry medium egg noodles
2 cups cooked chicken or turkey

In a 4 quart saucepan, combine broth, carrot, celery, onion, parsley, poultry seasoning and thyme. Heat to boiling, reduce heat to low and simmer 15 minutes. Add noodles. Cook 5 minutes or until vegetables and noodles are tender. Add chicken and heat through, stirring occasionally.

"Fast and filling! Students love it!"

Karen Barker   Prospect High School, Saratoga, CA

Fast 'n Easy Chili

Serves 6

1 $1/2$ pounds ground beef
1 envelope Lipton Recipe Secrets Onion Soup Mix*
1 (15 to 19 ounce) can red kidney or black beans, drained
1 $1/2$ cups water
1 (8 ounce) can tomato sauce
4 teaspoons chili powder
*Also terrific with Lipton Recipe Secrets Beefy Mushroom,
  Onion Mushroom or Beefy Onion Soup Mix

In 12" skillet, brown ground beef over medium-high heat; drain. Stir in remaining ingredients. Bring to a boil over high heat. Reduce heat to low and simmer, covered, stirring occasionally, about 20 minutes.

"An easy recipe to make on the go!"

Nancy Patten   Placerita Junior High School, Newhall, CA

Four-Bean Salsa Soup

Serves 6

$1/2$ pound kielbasa, cut into chunks
3 $1/2$ cups salsa or picante sauce
1 (15 ounce) can chili beans, undrained
1 (15 ounce) can black beans, undrained
1 (15 ounce) can white beans, undrained
1 (15 ounce) can kidney beans, undrained
$1/4$ cup cilantro, chopped
1 cup cheddar or jack cheese, shredded (optional)

In a large saucepan, sauté sausage 3 to 5 minutes over medium heat, stirring constantly. Add salsa, beans and cilantro. Stir and bring to a boil. Reduce heat, cover and simmer 5 to 10 minutes. Serve garnished with shredded cheese and additional cilantro, if desired.

"Hearty and flavorful! Add cornbread or tortillas for a complete meal."
Marguerite Smith   Murrieta Valley High School, Murrieta, CA

Garlic & Almond Gazpacho

Serves 6

1 honeydew melon, divided
$1/3$ cup almond meal or 2 ounces ground raw almonds
$1/3$ cup pine nuts
4 (large) cloves garlic, minced
1 teaspoon salt
4 slices country-style white bread, crusts removed, torn into pieces
6 tablespoons quality extra virgin olive oil
1 tablespoon + 1 teaspoon sherry vinegar (Spanish is best)
2 tablespoons white wine vinegar
4 cups iced water

Put the individual serving bowls in the freezer to chill. Cut melon in half; cut out four 1" cubes. Scoop remaining melon into balls and set aside. Place the four 1" melon cubes in blender along with remaining ingredients, except iced water and melon balls. Blend until smooth. Gradually blend in iced water on medium speed. Place 4 to 6 melon balls in each serving bowl and pour soup over top. Serve immediately.

"When I found this recipe, I thought I'd reached garlic heaven!
It's a Spanish recipe that I altered to fit my garlic lover's appetite."
Sandra Massey   Mt. View High School, El Monte, CA

Hamburger Soup

Serves 4 - 6

2 quarts water
1 teaspoon seasoned salt
$1/2$ teaspoon garlic salt
1 teaspoon onion powder
2 tablespoons beef bouillon
1 pound ground beef, browned
1 bay leaf
1 (medium) onion, chopped
4 potatoes, cubed
1 stalk celery, chopped
1 can green beans, cut
1 can corn
1 (5 ounce) can tomato sauce
1 cup mini carrots

Combine all ingredients in stock pot; bring to a boil. Reduce heat to a simmer. Simmer 45 minutes or longer.

"This is a quick meal. I keep frozen, cooked ground beef on hand. It takes minutes to combine all ingredients. While it's simmering, a quick bread can be prepared."

April Rosendahl   Chino High School, Chino, CA

Meatball Vegetable Soup

Serves 6 - 8

$2/3$ cup pasta shells, uncooked
4 cups chicken broth
1 (14.5 ounce) can diced tomatoes, undrained
1 (10.5 ounce) can condensed French onion soup, undiluted
15 Italian meatballs, frozen, fully cooked, thawed and quartered
1 $1/2$ cups fresh spinach, chopped
1 cup frozen carrots, sliced, thawed
$3/4$ cup canned kidney beans, rinsed and drained
$3/4$ cup garbanzo beans

Cook pasta according to package directions. Meanwhile, combine remaining ingredients in a large pot, bring to a boil, reduce heat. Cover and simmer 15 minutes or until vegetables are tender. Drain pasta and stir into soup.

"This soup is perfect for cold weather."

Astrid Curfman   Newcomb Academy, Long Beach, CA

Quick & Easy Chili

Serves Approx. 8

12 ounces ground beef
1 (medium) sweet onion, chopped
$1/2$ teaspoon garlic salt
1 (15.5 ounce) can kidney beans, drained
1 (15 ounce) can pinto beans, drained
1 (15 ounce) can black beans, drained
3 (10.75 ounce) cans Campbell's tomato soup
1 soup can of water
2 to 3 teaspoons chili powder

In large saucepan, brown ground beef with onion and garlic salt. Drain fat. Add all beans, soup, water, and chili powder. Bring to a boil and let simmer 20 minutes.

"You can garnish with cheese, crackers, sour cream, etc.
My family likes to put it over white rice."

Lori Wilson   A.B. Miller High School, Fontana, CA

Quick Kielbasa Soup

Serves 6 - 8

kielbasa, cooked
4 carrots, chopped
4 stalks celery, chopped
1 onion, chopped
5 cloves garlic, minced
4 cans chicken stock
4 cups water
1 (small) bag lentils

Cut and brown kielbasa in skillet and set aside. In same skillet, brown onion with garlic, carrots, and celery until softened; set aside. Bring stock and water to a boil and add lentils after rinsing. Add remaining ingredients an simmer 30 to 45 minutes. Add salt and pepper to taste.

"This is a quick and easy meal to serve on a cold day."

Sara D'Acquisto   Exeter High School, Exeter, CA

Quick Minestrone Soup

Serves 4 - 6

1 pound ground beef
1 onion, chopped
1 package onion soup mix
1 (16 ounce) can diced tomatoes
2 cans minestrone soup
3 cans water
1 can kidney beans, drained
1 cup pasta
1 1/2 cups cabbage, chopped
shredded cheese, sour cream

Brown ground beef; drain excess fat. Sauté onion. Add dry onion soup mix, tomatoes, soup, water and kidney beans; simmer 30 minutes. Add pasta and cabbage. Cook an additional 15 to 20 minutes. Serve hot, topped with shredded cheese and sour cream.

"Great veggie soup recipe from my friend, Ruth."

Millie Deeton   Ruben S. Ayala High School, Chino Hills, CA

Refried Bean Soup

Makes 7 cups

1 (small) onion, chopped
2 cloves garlic, minced
1 tablespoon vegetable oil
1 (31 ounce) can refried beans
1 (16 ounce) can diced tomatoes, undrained
1 (16 ounce) can diced tomatoes with green chiles, undrained
1 (14.5 ounce) can chicken broth
2 tablespoons fresh cilantro, chopped
crushed tortilla chips
2 cups Monterey jack cheese, shredded
1 cup sour cream

In stock pot, cook onion and garlic in oil over medium heat until tender. Add beans, both cans tomatoes and chicken broth. Bring to a boil, stirring constantly. Reduce heat and simmer 15 minutes. Stir in cilantro. Ladle soup into bowls. Top with tortilla chips, grated cheese and sour cream.

"Very quick and filling. Goes well with a plate of crudites.
Or don't add chips to soup and serve with chips and salsa."

Winn Yablonski   John F. Kennedy High School, La Palma, CA

Six-Can Chicken Tortilla Soup

Serves 6

1 (15 ounce) can whole kernel corn, drained
2 (14.5 ounce) cans chicken broth
1 (10 ounce) can chunk chicken
1 (15 ounce) can black beans
1 (10 ounce) can diced tomatoes with green chile peppers, drained
Toppings: Tortilla chips, shredded cheddar cheese

Open all cans and pour everything into a large saucepan or stockpot. Simmer over medium heat until chicken is heated through. Serve over tortilla chips and top with shredded cheddar cheese.

*"Delicious and easy. Throw away the cans and no one
will know that it's not from scratch!"*

Cari Sheridan   Grace Yokley Middle School, Ontario, CA

Taco Soup

Serves 6 - 8

1 pound hamburger, browned, drained
1 (large) can kidney beans
1 can mushrooms
2 (14.5 ounce) cans stewed tomatoes, cut up
2 (14.5 ounce) cans water
1 can black olives, sliced
1 (small) can tomato sauce
1 package Taco seasoning mix
Toppings: Corn chips, grated cheese, sour cream

Add all ingredients to a large pot. Heat through, being sure not to boil. Put soup in bowls; top with crushed corn chips, grated cheese and a dollop of sour cream.

"My family's favorite!"

Debi Spencer   Colton High School, Colton, CA

Thick and Hearty Chili

Serves 4

$3/4$ pound ground beef
1 cup onion, chopped
$1/2$ cup green pepper, chopped
2 cloves garlic, minced
1 (16 ounce) can tomatoes, cut up
1 (16 ounce) can kidney beans, drained
1 (8 ounce) can tomato sauce
2 to 3 teaspoons chili powder
$1/2$ teaspoon dried basil, crushed
$1/4$ teaspoon salt
$1/4$ teaspoon pepper

In a saucepan, brown ground beef with onion, green pepper and garlic; drain fat. Stir in undrained tomatoes, drained kidney beans, tomato sauce, chili powder, basil, salt and pepper. Bring to a boil. Cover and simmer 20 minutes.

"Easy fool-proof recipe! Prep and cook time is only about 35 minutes!"

Scott Domeny   Del Oro High School, Loomis, CA

Tortilla Soup with Beans

Serves 6

1 cup chicken, cooked, cubed
2 cups tomato sauce
1 $1/2$ cups water
8 ounces chunky salsa
1 cup whole kernel corn, drained
1 (16 ounce) can kidney beans, rinsed and drained
1 teaspoon dried oregano
1 teaspoon dried basil
1 (14 ounce) can chicken broth
1 clove garlic, minced
Optional: 1 cup grated cheese, sour cream, avocado, tortilla chips

Combine first 10 ingredients in a large saucepan; bring to a boil. Cover, reduce heat and simmer 12 minutes. If desired make a mound of cheese at the bottom of each serving bowl. Ladle soup over cheese, Garnish as desired.

"Easy and delicious. Can be made vegetarian by leaving out the chicken.
Also shredded or ground beef may be substituted for chicken."

Lynda Smith-Rains   Del Oro High School, Loomis, CA

Tortilla Soup

Serves 8-10

$^1/_2$ cup onion, chopped
$^1/_2$ teaspoon garlic, minced
4 tablespoons cilantro, chopped
2 (14 ounce) cans chicken broth
2 (small) cans tomato sauce
1 (14 ounce) can Mexican style stewed tomatoes
1 package taco seasoning mix
1 tablespoon Worcestershire sauce
4 boneless, skinless chicken breasts
salt and pepper, to taste
28 tortilla chips
small bag of frozen corn (optional)

Put all ingredients in a crock pot and cook on low for 8 to 9 hours. Remove chicken and shred before serving.

"This soup is tasty and very filling. Thanks to Darin Petzold and Dionne Bargabus for sharing the recipe."

Rhonda Nelson   Rancho Santa Margarita Intermediate School, RSM, CA

White Bean Chicken Chili

Serves 6

1 tablespoon olive oil
1 (small) onion
2 (medium) garlic cloves, peeled/chopped
1 (medium) red bell pepper chopped fine
2 (15 ounce) cans white beans, undrained
1 (4 ounce) can diced green chiles
$^1/_2$ teaspoon ground cumin
1 teaspoon chili powder
1 (14.5 ounce) can low sodium chicken broth
$^1/_2$ pound roasted chicken, cut in $^1/_2$" cubes
2 tablespoons lime juice
2 tablespoons cilantro, minced
6 tablespoons salsa (optional)
6 tablespoons sour cream (optional)

In a large pot heat the olive oil over medium heat. Add the onion, garlic and red pepper. Sauté 5 minutes. Stir in the white beans, chiles, cumin, chili powder and broth. Bring to a boil, reduce the heat and simmer 10 minutes. Stir in the chicken and simmer 5 minutes. Stir in the lime juice and cilantro. A tablespoon of salsa and sour cream can be used to garnish each serving of chili, if desired. Can also be made in the morning and left in crock pot on warm all day.

"I got this from my sister, Pam. Someone brought this into her office at Wells Fargo Bank. It's delicious."

Penny Childers   Ramona High School, Ramona, CA

White Chicken Chili

Serves 8

 2 boneless skinless chicken breasts
 2 cups water
 2 chicken bouillon cubes
 2 cans (or 7 ounces) chopped green chiles
 2 cans (or one 16 ounce bag frozen) white corn
 2 teaspoons cumin
 $1/2$ teaspoon ground pepper
 $1/4$ cup cilantro, finely chopped
 2 cans S&W brand white beans, liquid and all

Boil the chicken breasts in the water with the bouillon cubes. After chicken is cooked all the way through, remove it and cube it. Put the chicken and all of the other ingredients into the bouillon water. Cook over medium heat for 30 minutes on the stove or all day on low in the crock pot. Serve with sour cream, avocado, lime, sliced olives, grated cheese, and chopped tomatoes.

"This is the easiest and most delicious chili recipe ever! The toppings are what really make it great."

Nicole Rehmann   La Mesa Junior High School, Santa Clarita, CA

Yankee Chili

Serves 8 - 12

 1 $1/2$ pounds ground beef
 1 cup onion, chopped
 2 cloves garlic, minced
 1 (10.5 ounce) can beef broth
 2 (10.5 ounce) cans tomato soup
 1 soup can water
 1 can kidney beans, undrained
 1 can chili beans, undrained
 2 cups elbow macaroni
 2 tablespoons chili powder
 2 tablespoons vinegar
 grated cheddar cheese

In large saucepan, sauté ground beef with onion and garlic until browned. Add remaining ingredients, except cheese. Simmer 30 minutes, stirring occasionally. Top with cheese and serve.

"Serves a crowd! Cornbread as a side dish is a must!"

Joanne Montoy   Esperanza High School, Anaheim, CA

Salads Slaws *and* Dressings

Bean Salad

Serves 6 - 8

1 (16 ounce) can cut green beans
1 (16 ounce) can cut wax beans
1 (15 ounce) can dark red kidney beans
1 (16 ounce) can garbanzo beans
$1/2$ cup green pepper, chopped
$1/2$ cup sugar
$2/3$ cup vinegar
$1/3$ cup salad oil
1 teaspoon salt
$1/4$ teaspoon pepper

Drain beans of excess liquid and place in serving bowl with green pepper. In a small bowl, combine sugar, vinegar and salad oil; pour over drained beans. Season with salt and pepper and toss. Chill before serving.

"Best the next day!"

Pat Smith   Kern Valley High School, Lake Isabella, CA

Black Bean Salad

Serves 6-8

2 (15 ounce) cans black beans, rinsed and drained
1 (15 ounce) can corn, drained
1 onion, finely chopped
1 red pepper, diced
$1/2$ bunch cilantro, chopped
Your favorite Italian dressing

Place rinsed and well drained beans and corn in a serving bowl. Add chopped onion, diced red pepper, chopped cilantro, Italian dressing and toss. Refrigerate and serve.

Angela Croce   Mira Mesa High School, San Diego, CA

Blackberry Salad with Chicken

Serves 4

$1/4$ cup olive oil
$1/4$ cup honey
$1/4$ cup lemon juice
salt and pepper, to taste
4 ounces brie cheese
6 cups packaged baby greens (spring mix)
2 cups blackberries
1 cup (small) cherry tomatoes
$1/2$ cup pine nuts, toasted*
12 to 16 ounces roasted chicken breast, sliced $1/4$" thick

In a screw top jar, combine oil, honey, lemon juice, salt and pepper. Cover and shake well. Remove rind from cheese, if desired. Cut cheese into wedges. Place greens in individual salad bowls or on plates. Top with berries, tomatoes, pine nuts, brie and chicken slices. Drizzle with dressing. Serve immediately. Note: To roast pine nuts, place in a shallow baking pan and roast in a 350 degree oven 5 to 7 minutes, shaking pan once or twice. Watch closely so nuts don't burn.

"May substitute raspberries and/or strawberries for blackberries and you may substitute pork tenderloin or any meat or fish for the chicken."

Kathie Baczynski   Mt. Carmel High School, Poway, CA

Chicken Caesar Salad

Serves 4 - 5

1 package chopped romaine lettuce (from Costco)
   or 1 to 2 heads romaine, chopped
3 to 4 Mesquite chicken breasts
Parmesan cheese, freshly grated
Girards Caesar dressing
croutons (optional)

Put lettuce in large bowl. Warm up chicken on barbecue or George Foreman grill. Slice or cube chicken breast and add to salad greens. Add desired amount of cheese, dressing and croutons. Toss and serve.

"Very quick and easy, thanks to prepackaged foods. This is a favorite at our house."

Karen Frey   Galena High School, Reno, NV

Chinese Chicken Salad

Serves 4

2 cups Romaine lettuce, torn
2 cups iceberg lettuce, torn
$^1/_4$ bunch cilantro, chopped
1 cup cooked chicken, cubed
$^1/_2$ cup red bell pepper, chopped
1 avocado, peeled, sliced, cubed
1 (11 ounce) can Mandarin oranges, drained
$^1/_2$ cup cashews
$^1/_2$ cup chow mein noodles
2 tablespoons vegetable oil
2 tablespoons rice wine vinegar
1 clove garlic, minced
1 teaspoon fresh ginger, finely chopped
2 teaspoons soy sauce
2 teaspoons sesame oil

Toss together greens and cilantro in serving bowl. Then top with chicken, bell pepper, avocado, oranges, cashews and noodles. Whisk remaining ingredients together and pour over salad. Toss before serving.

Patty Stroming   **Mitchell Senior Elementary, Atwater, CA**

Chinese Macaroni Salad

Serves 8 - 10

2 cups salad macaroni, cooked
$^1/_2$ cup vegetable oil
1 onion, finely diced
1 green pepper, finely diced
1 (15 ounce) mushrooms, sliced, drained
2 cups cooked chicken, chopped
3 ribs celery, finely diced
$^1/_2$ cup soy sauce

Mix all ingredients together. Serve warm or cold.

"In the time it takes to cook the macaroni, you can have the rest of the ingredients prepared. It's a snap. Great to take to a pot luck."

Barbara Correia   **Foothill High School, Pleasanton, CA**

Crab Louis

Serves 4

    1 (medium) head leaf lettuce
    1 (medium) head iceberg lettuce
    8 ounces package crabmeat, flaked
    2 (large) tomatoes, cut into wedges
    3 eggs, hard cooked, sliced
    2 lemons, cut into wedges
    1 cup mayonnaise
    3 tablespoons chili sauce
    1 tablespoon green pepper, chopped
    1 teaspoon pimiento, chopped
    1 teaspoon chives, chopped
    dash paprika
    1 bell pepper, sliced

Line platter with leaf lettuce. Tear iceberg lettuce into bite-sized pieces and place atop lettuce leaves. Arrange flaked crabmeat, tomato wedges, eggs and lemon wedges on top of lettuce. Combine mayonnaise with chili sauce, chopped green peppers, pimento and green onion; drizzle over crabmeat. Sprinkle with paprika. Garnish with bell pepper slices.

Patty Stroming   Mitchell Senior Elementary, Atwater, CA

Crisp Cucumber in Dill Dressing

Serves 6

    $1/_4$ cup red wine vinegar
    1 teaspoon sugar
    $1/_2$ teaspoon salt
    $1/_2$ teaspoon pepper
    2 tablespoons olive oil
    2 cups cucumbers, sliced
    1 cup red onion, sliced, rings separated
    2 (medium) tomatoes, cut into wedges

In a large bowl, stir together vinegar, sugar, salt, pepper and olive oil. Add cucumbers, onion and tomatoes; toss to coat. Let stand 15 minutes before serving.

"Unusually delicious!"

Anne Hawes   Cottonwood High School, Murray, UT

Five-Cup Fruit Salad

Serves 8 - 12

1 cup Mandarin orange pieces, drained
1 cup coconut, shredded
1 cup miniature marshmallows
1 cup pineapple chunks, drained
1 cup whipping or sour cream

Mix together and allow to set at least 3 hours before serving. May be made up to 24 hours ahead.

"For color, I add halved Maraschino cherries."

Laurie Giauque   Olympus High School, Salt Lake City, UT

Mandarin Pasta Salad

Serves 12

Dressing:
1 teaspoon fresh ginger root, peeled, finely chopped
1 clove garlic, pressed
$1/3$ cup rice vinegar
$1/4$ cup orange juice
$1/4$ cup vegetable oil
1 teaspoon sesame oil
1 envelope dry onion soup mix
2 teaspoons sugar
Salad:
8 ounces bow tie pasta
$1/2$ cucumber, scored, seeded, sliced
$1/2$ cup red bell pepper, diced
$1/2$ cup red onion, coarsely chopped
1 (6 ounce) package fresh baby spinach leaves
1 (11 ounce) can Mandarin orange segments, drained
2 cups chicken, cooked, diced
$1/2$ cup almonds, sliced, toasted
nonstick cooking spray

Prepare dressing: In a small bowl whisk dressing ingredients together; set aside. *Prepare salad:* Cook pasta according to package directions; drain and rinse under cold running water. Place in large bowl. Meanwhile, combine prepared vegetables with chicken and almonds; add to pasta. Pour dressing over salad and toss. Serve immediately. Note: To toast sliced almonds, place in a frying pan over medium heat. Spray almonds with a nonstick cooking spray so they don't stick to each other. Stir occasionally until golden brown.

"When pressed for time, buy a roasted chicken at the deli, cut it up
and serve in the salad as directed. This usually yields 1 + cups per pound
and is more economical than chicken breasts. If you buy them at Sam's Club
or Costco, they are bigger and cost even less!"

Kelly Smith   Las Vegas High School, Las Vegas, NV

Mediterranean Pasta Salad

Serves 4   **(Photo opposite page 97)**

3/4 pound peppered pork roast, cooked, cut into thin strips
12 ounces penne or ziti pasta, cooked, drained
1 (small) cucumber, diced
6 ounces feta cheese, crumbled
1 cup cherry tomatoes, halved
1/2 cup fresh mint leaves, chopped
1/2 cup Greek vinaigrette dressing

In large bowl, gently toss all ingredients with dressing. Serve on shallow salad bowls or dinner plates.

National Pork Board   **www.theotherwhitemeat.com**

Now Why Didn't I Think Of That Salad

Serves 2

1/2 head lettuce (or your favorite mix of pre-washed greens)
1 tomato, cut into wedges
1 bell pepper, seeded, sliced into chunks
1 avocado, peeled, pit removed, cut into chunks
2 to 4 green onions, sliced
2 hamburger patties, seasoned, cooked
balsamic vinaigrette salad dressing

Prepare 2 large bowls of salad while hamburger patties are grilling or broiling. Place a cooked hamburger patty in the middle of each salad and sprinkle vinaigrette over all.

"The warm meat slightly wilts the greens and the vinaigrette seasons it all. Talk about fast and healthy!"

Larkin Evans   **Half Moon Bay High School, Half Moon Bay, CA**

Orange-Cream Fruit Salad

Serves 10

1 (20-ounce) can pineapple chunks, drained
1 (16-ounce) can peach slices, drained
1 (11-ounce) mandarin orange sections, drained
3 (medium) bananas
2 (medium) apples cored. and chopped
1 (3.5 or 3.75 ounce) package instant vanilla pudding
1 1/2 cups milk
3 ounces (1/3 cup) frozen orange juice concentrate
3/4 cup sour cream
lettuce cups

In large bowl, combine pineapple chunks, peaches, orange sections, bananas, and apples; set aside. In small bowl combine dry pudding mix, milk, and orange juice concentrate. Beat 1 to 2 minutes or until well blended. Beat in sour cream. Fold into the fruit mixture. Cover and refrigerate several hours. Serve the salad in lettuce cups on individual serving plates. Note: If you want to make this up a day in advance, add bananas just before serving.

"This salad tastes like a 50/50 ice cream bar."

Renee Paulsin   Hemet High School, Hemet, CA

Quick Caesar Salad

Serves 6 - 8

1 (large) head romaine lettuce
1 cup (4 ounces) Parmesan cheese, shredded
$1/2$ box seasoned croutons (Mrs. Cubbisons)
1 (8 ounce) bottle Cardini's Caesar Dressing

Combine lettuce, cheese and croutons in large salad bowl; toss with Cardini's Original Caesar dressing just before serving.

"This is a favorite wherever I take it. The dressing is the secret!"

Gerry Fairbanks   Bingham High School, South Jordan, UT

Quick Jello Salad

Serves 4 - 6

1 pint small curd cottage cheese
1 (8 ounce) container Cool Whip
1 (8 ounce) can pineapple, crushed, drained
1 (3 ounce) package jello (dry)

Combine all ingredients in a bowl and chill. Ready to serve in $1/2$ hour!

"You can use different flavors/colors of jello to fit any holiday."

Ruth Schletewitz   Rafer Johnson Junior High School, Kingsburg, CA

Savory Spinach Salad

Serves 4 - 6

1 package baby spinach
1 $1/2$ cups strawberries, sliced
1 bottle Marie's Poppy Seed Dressing
1 chicken breast, grilled, sliced

Rinse spinach leaves; dry and place in serving bowl. Add sliced strawberries and toss gently. Add enough dressing, to taste, and toss. Place chicken slices on top and serve.

"Delicious, colorful salad for an entree or side dish."

Teresa Hayes   Buena High School, Ventura, CA

Sesame Cole Slaw

Serves 8

3 cups cabbage, thinly sliced
1 1/2 cups carrots, shredded
1 cup spinach, thinly sliced
1/4 cup rice vinegar
2 tablespoons sugar
1 tablespoon fresh ginger, peeled, finely chopped
2 teaspoons toasted dark sesame oil
1 teaspoon soy sauce
salt and freshly ground pepper, to taste

In a large bowl, mix together the vegetables. In a small bowl, whisk together the vinegar, sugar, ginger, oil and soy sauce. Toss dressing with vegetables and season with salt and pepper. Chill at least 1 hour before serving.

Millie Deeton   Ruben S. Ayala High School, Chino Hills, CA

Spinach Salad with Strawberries

Serves 2 - 4

1 (12 ounce) bag baby spinach
1 to 2 baskets strawberries, sliced
Raspberry Poppyseed Dressing, fat free & oil free
slivered almonds, lightly toasted

Place spinach in a salad bowl. Add strawberries. Pour desired amount of salad dressing; toss. Sprinkle with almonds and serve.

"Kozlowski Farms Sonoma County Classics Raspberry Poppyseed Dressing is available at Bristol Farms or use Brianna's Home Style Blush Wine Vinaigrette Strawberry Dressing. "

Becky Oppen   Dana Hills High School, Dana Point, CA

Strawberry Spinach Salad

Serves 4 - 6

$1/4$ cup almonds, sliced
1 $1/2$ cups strawberries, sliced
$1/2$ cup cucumber, cubed
$1/4$ cup red onion, diced
1 package baby spinach
Dressing:
1 lemon, juiced
2 tablespoons white wine vinegar
$1/3$ cup sugar
1 tablespoon vegetable oil
1 teaspoon poppy seeds

Toss together almonds, strawberries, cucumber, red onion and baby spinach. Mix juiced lemon, white wine vinegar, sugar, oil and poppy seeds. Pour dressing over salad when ready to serve.

Rebecca Hutchings   Spring Valley High School, Las Vegas, NV

Tabouli

Serves 5

$1/2$ cup boiling water
1 $1/4$ cups dry couscous
6 tablespoons olive oil
$1/3$ cup lemon juice
2 cloves garlic, minced
1 (large) tomato, diced
4 green onions, chopped
1 (small) cucumber, diced
4 tablespoons fresh parsley, chopped
$1/2$ cup almonds, chopped
1 tablespoon mint, chopped (optional)
$1/2$ cup feta cheese (optional)

Mix boiling water with dry couscous. Add olive oil, lemon juice and garlic; stir well. Cover and let sit at least 5 minutes. Fluff with fork. Add tomato, green onion, cucumber, parsley, almonds and mint. Chill at least 15 minutes or up to overnight. Garnish with feta cheese and serve chilled.

"I double this recipe and take it to gatherings. I have a box of couscous from Trader Joe's in my pantry ready in case I need a quick salad."

Val Poalillo   Paso Robles High School, Paso Robles, CA

Thai Beef Salad

Serves 4

1 (small) head romaine lettuce
4 leaves red leaf lettuce
1 head Belgian endive
$3/4$ cup oil, divided
$1/4$ cup fresh lime juice, divided
3 tablespoons soy sauce, divided
1 pound beef, cut into thin strips
1 (1" piece) fresh ginger root, grated
1 tablespoon brown sugar
2 cloves garlic, minced
3 jalapeños, minced
$1/4$ cup cilantro, chopped
3 tomatoes, cut into wedges
2 green onions, chopped

Tear greens into bite-size pieces. In small bowl, combine 2 tablespoons each oil, lime juice, and soy sauce. Add beef, stir, and marinate at least 20 minutes at room temperature. In food processor, combine $1/2$ cup oil, 2 tablespoons lime juice, 1 tablespoon soy sauce, ginger, brown sugar, garlic and jalapeños; purée. Reserve marinade. Stir-fry beef in 2 tablespoons oil until just browned. Mix reserved marinade with dressing. Top greens with beef; pour dressing into wok and stir to heat and mix in beef juices. Pour hot dressing over salad. Add cilantro, tomatoes, and green onions; toss.

"Fast, healthy and spicy! Switch lettuces to save costs."

Priscilla Burns   Pleasant Valley High School, Chico, CA

Thai Chicken Salad

Serves 6

$3/4$ cup canola oil
1 tablespoon sesame oil
$1/3$ cup honey
$1/4$ cup lime juice
1 teaspoon apple cider vinegar
2 tablespoons soy sauce
2 tablespoons peanut butter
1 clove garlic, crushed
1 teaspoon fresh ginger, peeled, grated (2" piece)
1 red or green chile, seeds removed, finely chopped (optional)
1 teaspoon black pepper
3 cups lettuce mix
8 ounces grilled chicken, shredded, or cut into strips
1 cup cilantro, chopped
6 cups Napa cabbage, finely shredded
6 green onions, finely sliced
$1/4$ cup roasted peanuts, chopped (optional)

Blend first 11 ingredients in the blender or food processor. Add dressing to remaining salad ingredients; toss and serve.

Betty Rabin-Fung   Sierra Vista Junior High School, Santa Clarita, CA

Tropical Banana Citrus Ambrosia

Serves 4 - 6

1 (8 ounce) container whipped topping
1 (large) box banana instant pudding
1 (large) can crushed pineapple
1 (large) can Mandarin oranges, drained or 2 fresh
2 cups miniature marshmallows
4 ounces nuts, chopped

Combine whipped topping and banana pudding; stir well until thoroughly blended. Add pineapple and Mandarin oranges. Fold in marshmallow and nuts. Refrigerate 30 minutes.

"You can also add grated chocolate and coconut.
This makes a great topping for angel food or pound cake."

Marleigh Williams   Corning High School, Corning, CA

Sauces Salsas *and* Marinades

Citrus Sauce
Makes 2 cups

2 tablespoons flour
$1/2$ cup sugar
$1/8$ teaspoon salt
$1/2$ lemon, juice and rind
1 orange, juice and rind
1 tablespoon butter
$1/2$ pint whipping cream
1 angel food cake, sliced

Combine flour, sugar and salt. Juice lemon and orange, then grate rind of each. Combine flour mixture and citrus mixture; add butter. Cook over medium heat until thickened. Chill over dish of ice or in refrigerator. Whip the cream, then fold into cooked citrus mixture. Serve dollops over angel food cake slices.

"Love this sauce on just about any dessert! Keeps in refrigerator for a day or two."
Pat Johnson   Iron Horse Middle School, San Ramon, CA

Sweet and Sour Sauce
Makes 1 cup

2 tablespoons + 2 teaspoons rice vinegar
$1/2$ cup water
$1/4$ cup + 2 tablespoons granulated sugar
pinch salt
pinch white pepper
2 drops Tabasco sauce
1 tablespoon cornstarch
1 tablespoon cold water
1 tablespoon ketchup
$1/4$ teaspoon fresh ginger, minced

In a small sauce pan over medium heat, bring vinegar, water, sugar, salt, pepper and Tabasco to a boil. In a small bowl mix cornstarch and cold water.

Add the cornstarch slurry to the boiling mixture, and cook until thick and bubbly. Remove from heat and add the ketchup and ginger.

"This sauce is like what you would get at the restaurant, but better.
Bake some chicken nuggets and have sweet and sour chicken.
You can add pineapple chunks and diced green pepper if you like."

Shauna Young   Jordan High School, Sandy, UT

Vicki's Meat Rub

Makes about 1 cup

> 1 cup brown sugar
> 3 tablespoons kosher salt
> 1 tablespoon chili powder
> $1/2$ teaspoon pepper
> $1/2$ teaspoon cumin
> $1/2$ teaspoon cayenne pepper
> $1/2$ teaspoon paprika

Mix all ingredients together. Rub into meat and let stand 20 minutes to 3 hours. Use rubber gloves as it can stain hands. The spices can be doubled if you want it spicy. This recipe can be doubled and stored in a container for later use. This rub is best when cooking on a grill or rotisserie.

"My friend, Vicki, uses this rub on her favorites—baby back ribs,
roast and pork chops."

Mary Springhorn   Anderson High School, Anderson, CA

20-Minute Tamale Pie

Serves 6 - 8

    1 onion, finely chopped
    1 pound ground beef
    2 tablespoons butter
    1 (16 ounce) can stewed tomatoes
    1 (17 ounce) can whole kernel corn, undrained
    1 cup sour cream
    1 cup cornmeal
    1 (4.5 ounce) can olives, chopped
    2 teaspoons salt
    1 tablespoon chili powder
    1 tablespoon Accent
    $1/2$ teaspoon cumin
    2 cups jack cheese, shredded

In a 12" skillet, sauté onion with ground beef and butter. Add tomatoes, corn, sour cream, cornmeal, olives and seasonings, stirring until thoroughly blended. Sprinkle with cheese. Cover and simmer 20 minutes. Serve with flour tortillas.

"This recipe was given to me by my sister-in-law, and it's truly kid friendly!"
Joanne Montoy   Esperanza High School, Anaheim, CA

Baked Meatballs

Serves 6 - 8

1 $1/2$ pounds lean ground beef
$1/2$ cup rolled oats
2 eggs, slightly beaten
$1/2$ cup onion, finely chopped
$1/4$ cup milk
1 teaspoon salt
dash pepper
1 teaspoon Worcestershire sauce

Preheat oven to 350 degrees. Combine all ingredients; mix well. Form into about 20 balls about the size of a large walnut or use a cookie dough scoop. Place on foil-lined baking pan. Bake 30 to 45 minutes.

"Tastes great when served with spaghetti or any noodles and sauce."

Cheryl Moyle   Olympus High School, Salt Lake City, UT

BBQ Hamburger Crispies

Serves 4 - 6

1 pound ground beef
1 egg
1 cup crisp rice cereal, divided
1 teaspoon salt
$1/4$ teaspoon pepper
1 tablespoon onion, finely chopped
3 tablespoons brown sugar
$1/2$ cup catsup
$1/8$ teaspoon nutmeg
1 teaspoon dry mustard

Preheat oven to 400 degrees. Combine ground beef with egg, $3/4$ cup cereal, salt, pepper and onion; mix well. Mix brown sugar, catsup, nutmeg and mustard to make a sauce. Add half of the sauce to the meat mixture; mix well. Shape meat into 6 large meatballs or 12 smaller meatballs. Place in 3" muffin pans or a baking dish. Top meatballs with remaining sauce and sprinkle with remaining $1/4$ cup cereal. Bake about 30 minutes.

"This is simply delicious and so easy. It's a great recipe for the kids to make. Serve with vegetables and a salad."

Kathleen Fresquez   Mountain View High School, El Monte, CA

Beef and Rice Tortilla Pie

Serves 2

$1/2$ pound ground beef
$1/4$ cup onion, chopped
1 teaspoon garlic, minced
1 can enchilada sauce
$1/2$ cup black olives, sliced
$1/2$ teaspoon cumin
1 cup rice, cooked
2 flour tortillas
1 cup cheddar cheese, grated
2 green onions, chopped
1 (small) tomato, chopped
lettuce, shredded
sour cream, guacamole, if desired

Preheat oven to 350 degrees. Sauté meat with onion and garlic until cooked through; drain excess liquid. Add enchilada sauce, olives and cumin; simmer 2 minutes. Add rice and mix well. In a well oiled 8" pie pan, spoon a thin layer of rice mixture and cover with a tortilla. Layer half of the remaining rice and half of the cheese over tortilla. Repeat layers of tortilla, rice and cheese. Top with onion and tomato. Bake 20 to 30 minutes. Serve on a bed of lettuce; garnish with sour cream and guacamole, if desired.

Linnea Howe   Pacifica High School, Oxnard, CA

Beef or Pork Carolina

Serves 4 - 6

2 (medium) onions, sliced
1 (4 to 6 pound) shoulder roast, or pork butt, or ribs
2 tablespoons brown sugar
$1/2$ tablespoon paprika
$1/4$ cup cider vinegar
4 teaspoons Worcestershire sauce
1 $1/2$ teaspoons crushed red pepper flakes
1 $1/2$ teaspoons sugar
$1/2$ teaspoon dry mustard
$1/2$ teaspoon garlic salt
$1/4$ teaspoon cayenne pepper

Crockpot RECIPE!

Place sliced onions in crock pot; top with meat, then remaining ingredients. Cook on low temperature 10 hours or high heat for 6 hours.

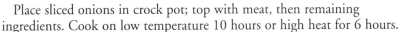

"You can shred meat and put on hamburger buns and cover with sauce from crockpot; or serve meat with rice or potatoes, tortillas or beans. It's an easy and delicious recipe from my mom."

Kristine Carlin   Laguna Middle School, San Luis Obispo, CA

California Tamale Casserole

Serves 4

$1/3$ cup yellow cornmeal
$3/4$ cup milk
1 egg, beaten
$1/2$ pound ground beef
2 tablespoons chili seasoning mix
1 teaspoon salt
$1/2$ (16 ounce) can tomatoes (1 cup)
$1/2$ (17 ounce) can whole kernel corn
$1/4$ cup black olives
$1/4$ cup cheddar cheese, shredded

Preheat oven to 375 degrees. Mix cornmeal, milk and egg; set aside. Brown meat in skillet, stirring to crumble; drain fat. Add chili seasoning mix, salt, tomatoes, corn and olives to meat; mix well. Stir into cornmeal mixture. Pour into a greased 8" x 8" baking dish and bake 35 minutes.

"My advanced Foods students love this recipe.
It's something they can make during a foods lab."

Charlotte Runyan   Saddleback High School, Santa Ana, CA

Cornbread Casserole

Makes 6 Servings

$1/2$ cup onion
$1/2$ cup green pepper
1 pound ground beef
1 (15.5 ounce) can mild chili beans, in sauce
$3/4$ cup barbecue sauce
$1/2$ teaspoon salt
1 (8.5 ounce) package corn muffin mix
1 (11 ounce) can Mexican-style corn, drained

Preheat oven to 400. Chop onion and bell pepper. Cook ground beef, adding onion and pepper. Drain. Stir in chili beans, barbecue sauce and salt. Bring to a boil. Pour into a square baking dish. In a separate bowl, prepare muffin mix according to the package and stir in corn. Spoon over meat mixture and spread evenly. Bake 30 minutes.

"When I make this for little children I omit the onion and pepper
and use a little onion powder instead. It's a favorite at our house!"

Daphne Stockdale   Riverton High School, Riverton, UT

Cowboy Delight
Serves 6

 1 pound ground beef
 1 teaspoon chili powder
 1 teaspoon garlic powder
 1 teaspoon salt
 $1/2$ teaspoon pepper
 1 can cream of mushroom soup
 1 can tomato soup
 1 $1/2$ cups macaroni or angel hair pasta

Combine ground beef, chili powder, garlic, salt and pepper in a frying pan and cook until done. While browning the beef, cook pasta according to package directions. Add soups and pasta to ground beef mixture. Cook over medium heat until bubbly. Serve.

Daphne Stockdale   Riverton High School, Riverton, UT

Easy Lasagna Casserole
Serves 4

 1 pound ground beef
 salt and pepper, to taste
 1 tablespoon sugar
 2 (8 ounce) cans tomato sauce
 1 (8 ounce) package egg noodles
 1 cup sour cream
 1 (small) package cream cheese
 1 to 2 tablespoons green onion, chopped or dry minced onion
 $1/2$ to 1 cup cheddar cheese, grated

Preheat oven to 375 degrees. Brown and season ground beef to taste with salt and pepper. Add sugar and tomato sauce. Simmer 15 minutes. Cook noodles & drain. Mix sour cream, cream cheese and onion in small bowl. Layer noodles, sour cream mixture, then tomato and meat mixture in casserole dish. Top with grated cheese and bake 10 to 15 minutes or until heated through.

"This is an easy lasagna that has a great flavor."

Camille Hicks   Riverton High School, Riverton, UT

Easy Microwave Meatloaf
Serves 6

> 1 (8 ounce) can tomato sauce, divided
> $1/4$ cup brown sugar
> 1 teaspoon prepared mustard
> 2 eggs, lightly beaten
> 1 (medium) onion, minced
> $1/4$ cup cracker crumbs
> 2 pounds lean ground beef
> 1 $1/2$ teaspoons salt
> $1/4$ teaspoon pepper

In small bowl, combine tomato sauce, brown sugar, and mustard. Set aside. In large mixing bowl, combine eggs, onion, cracker crumbs, ground beef, salt, and pepper. Add $1/2$ cup of tomato sauce mixture and stir thoroughly. Place meat mixture in glass ring mold, or 2-quart microwave-proof round casserole. Pour remaining tomato sauce over top of meat. Cook, uncovered, on high, 12 to 14 minutes. Let stand, covered, 5 to 10 minutes before serving.

"Meatloaf can take an hour to cook in the oven. This recipe takes 12 to 14 minutes! To create a ring mold, turn a glass upside down and place in middle of round casserole dish, then place meat mixture around the glass."

Debra Warren   Hueneme High School, Oxnard, CA

French Dip
Serves 6-8

> 1 cross rib roast
> 16 ounces water (enough to cover roast)
> 1 package Lipton Beefy Onion Soup
> Rolls, (any hard roll will work)

Place roast in the crock pot. Sprinkle Lipton soup over top and add water. Cover crock pot with lid. Cook on low for 8 to 10 hours. When roast is completely cooked, remove from crockpot and cool slightly; cut into bite size pieces. Place roast in sliced rolls. Strain juice in crock pot to make the au jus. Serve au jus in small cups or bowls. Dip sandwich as desired. Enjoy!

"This is one of my absolute favorites. This French dip recipe is quick and easy for any one with a busy schedule."

Katie Borgmeier   Riverton High School, Riverton, UT

60

Fritoli Casserole

Serves 4 - 6

3 cups corn chips, divided
1 pound ground beef
1/4 cup onion, minced
1 (15.5 ounce) can chili beans
1 (2.25 ounce) can sliced olives
1 tablespoon water
1/2 teaspoon salt
1 1/2 cups sharp cheddar cheese, shredded, divided

Preheat oven to 350 degrees. Place 2 cups corn chips in a 1 1/2 quart casserole. Brown ground beef with onion in a skillet. Add undrained chili beans, olives, water, salt and half of the cheese. Mix well and spread over chips in casserole dish. Sprinkle with remaining cheese and chips. Bake 30 minutes.

"Simple and quickly assembled. Relax while it bakes or fold your laundry!"

Kathleen Fresquez   Mountain View High School, El Monte, CA

Gooey Tacos

Serves 4 - 6

1 pound ground beef
1 onion, diced
1 clove garlic, diced
1 can refried beans
1 can Mexican-style stewed tomatoes
1 can tomato sauce
cheese, grated
tortillas
salsa
lettuce, shredded
tomatoes, chopped

Fry ground beef with onion and garlic, breaking up until cooked completely. Stir in refried beans, stewed tomatoes and tomato sauce, mashing and mixing until ingredients are mixed; keep on medium-low heat to simmer. Stir in a little bit of shredded cheese. Prepare tortillas; keep warm. Place a few tablespoons meat mixture on a tortilla, add desired amounts of cheese, salsa, lettuce, tomatoes, hot sauce - whatever you fancy!

"A family recipe enjoyed by all!"

Connie Signs   Burney Junior High School, Burney, CA

Ground Beef Cheesy Noodle Casserole

Serves 4

> 1 pound ground beef
> 2 cloves garlic, minced
> 1 teaspoon salt
> dash pepper
> $1/2$ teaspoon sugar
> 1 (medium) can tomato sauce
> 6 ounces egg noodles
> 1 (4 ounce) package cream cheese
> 6 green onions, chopped
> 1 cup sour cream
> $1/4$ cup sharp cheddar cheese, shredded

Preheat oven to 350 degrees. Brown beef; drain fat. Add next 5 ingredients and simmer. Cook noodles; drain. Mix cream cheese with green onion and sour cream in a small bowl. Add cheese mixture to hot, drained noodles and mix well. In a 9" pan, alternate layers of sauce and noodles. Top with shredded cheese. Bake 20 minutes.

"My husband's favorite comfort casserole."

Janet Tingley   Atascadero High School, Atascadero, CA

Ground Beef Delight

Serves 4 - 6

> 1 pound ground beef
> $1/2$ onion, chopped
> 1 can cream of mushroom soup
> 1 can cream of chicken soup
> 1 cup evaporated milk
> 1 cup water
> 5 carrots, peeled and sliced
> 3 to 4 potatoes, peeled and cut into cubes
> $1/4$ to $1/2$ cup celery, chopped (optional)

Preheat oven to 350 degrees. Brown and season the ground beef and onions; drain. Mix soups, milk, and water together and add to ground beef. Place vegetables in baking dish. Pour meat and sauce mixture over the vegetables. Bake, uncovered, 1 $1/2$ hours.

"The evaporated milk give this a great flavor. It is easy to put together and works well in a crock pot or slow cooker on low for 4 to 6 hours until vegetables are soft."

Camille Hicks   Riverton High School, Riverton, UT

Kell's Shepard's Pie with Ulster Champ Topping

Serves 6 - 8

Shepard's Pie:
1 1/2 pounds ground free-range beef
1/2 cup sweet onion, diced
1/2 cup baby carrots, diced
1 to 2 teaspoons garlic, minced or pressed
1/4 cup Guinness draught stout
1/4 cup cabernet wine
7 ounces (3/4 cup plus 2 tablespoons) beef broth
1 teaspoon Worcestershire sauce
1/4 teaspoon each: dried basil, dried oregano,
    dried sage and dried marjoram
1 cup peas, preferably fresh or frozen, thawed
2 tablespoons butter
2 tablespoons flour
1/2 teaspoon salt
1/4 teaspoon pepper
Ulster Champ Topping:
1 1/4 pounds russet potatoes (about 4 medium), scrubbed, peeled
4 tablespoons butter
1 cup Irish white cheddar cheese, finely grated
1/4 cup milk
1/4 cup fresh parsley, finely minced
1/3 cup scallions or chives, chopped
salt and white pepper, to taste

Brown ground beef in a Dutch oven or other heavy sauce pot over low to moderate heat. Allow to simmer until cooked through, about 5 to 10 minutes. Drain excess fat and add onion, carrots, garlic, stout, wine, broth, Worcestershire and spices. Stir and bring to a simmer over low heat. Cook 15 minutes or until carrots are fork tender. Add peas. While meat is simmering, bring large pot of water to boil for potatoes.

Meanwhile, in small saucepan, melt butter and stir in flour to make a roux. Slowly incorporate roux into simmering beef mixture until desired thickness is achieved. (If mixture is simmered too long or cooked over too high heat, less roux is needed.) Continue to cook 5 to 10 minutes to allow roux and flavors to meld. Season with salt and pepper. Remove to a 9 1/2" round casserole dish or deep pie dish. Preheat oven to 350 degrees and begin preparing topping. Cut potatoes into large pieces. Simmer in boiling water until fork tender. Drain well and return to pot to low heat to remove excess moisture. Stir in butter and cheese and whip, gradually adding milk, parsley, and scallions or chives. Season with salt and pepper. Spoon potato topping evenly over meat mixture making irregular peaks with the back of a spoon. Alternately, use a pastry bag and star tip to pipe potatoes over meat mixture. Bake 20 to 30 minutes or until potatoes are golden brown and crusty on edges and mixture is heated through. If desired, place casserole under broiler

1 to 2 minutes to crisp potato topping. Remove from oven, allow to cool slightly to set and serve immediately from casserole dish. Serve with HP Sauce (Irish-English steak-style sauce), steak sauce or pan gravy, if desired. Note: Pie can be cooked and served in individual baking dishes. Adjust final baking time as needed.

"This recipe was written up in the Press Enterprise. Kell's Irish Restaurant is in Portland, Oregon. It takes a bit of time but soooo worth it! The Irish cheddar cheese is found in the deli or specialized food sections. It is a delight to the taste buds!"

Judith Topp   A.B. Miller High School, Fontana, CA

Kirsten's Crockpot Tacos

Serves 4 - 6

1 chuck roast
2 red, yellow, or orange bell peppers, chopped
1 white onion, chopped
1 (14 ounce) can Mexican-style tomatoes, diced
1 cup salsa

Place all ingredients in order in a crockpot. Cook on high or about 5 to 6 hours. Serve with tortillas, beans, rice and cheese.

"My students always enrich my life in so many ways. Kirsten wanted to share her favorite dish with me that she created herself. It has become a favorite of mine too! So quick to make before work. Thanks Kirsten!"

Brenda Burke   Mt. Whitney High School, Visalia, CA

Macho Nacho Supreme

Serves 8 - 10

1 1/2 pounds ground beef
1 package hot taco seasoning
2 (16 ounce) cans black refried beans
1 (16 ounce) jar salsa
1 cup onion, chopped
1/2 pound cheddar cheese, grated
1 (large) bag tortilla chips
Garnish: Chopped tomato; sour cream; guacamole

Preheat oven to 350 degrees. Brown ground beef; drain fat. Stir in taco seasoning and mix well. In large pan, heat together refried black beans and salsa. Add ground beef mixture and heat thoroughly. Place mixture into a 9" x 13" oven-safe casserole dish. Layer with chopped onions and grated cheese. Place in oven for 30 minutes or until cheese is melted. Serve over tortilla chips and garnish with chopped tomatoes, sour cream and guacamole, as desired.

"Quick, inexpensive dish for unexpected company or family gatherings."

Judy Dobkins   Redlands High School, Redlands, CA

Turkey & Black Bean Wrap

Makes 8 wraps

 2 (medium) tomatoes, chopped
 $1/2$ cup black beans, rinsed, drained
 4 tablespoons diced green chiles
 $1/3$ cup green onions, sliced
 1 tablespoon fresh cilantro, chopped
 water
 1 (1.27 ounce) package Lawry's Fajitas Spices & Seasonings
 3 cups turkey, cooked, shredded or diced
 8 (large) Mission flour tortillas, warmed to soften

In medium bowl, combine tomatoes, black beans, chiles, green onion and cilantro; set aside. In large skillet, stir together water and Fajitas Spices & Seasonings; bring to a boil. Stir in turkey and reduce heat to low. Mix in tomato mixture and cook on low for 5 minutes or until turkey is thoroughly cooked, stirring occasionally. Scoop $1/2$ cup filling on each tortilla. Fold in sides and roll up to enclose filling. Note: Substitute cooked chicken or pork for turkey.

Lawry's Foods, Inc.   www.lawrys.com

Ready in 30 Minutes!

Weeknight Meatball Stew

Serves 4

12 ounces frozen fully-cooked beef meatballs (about 23 meatballs)
1 jar (11 ounces) beef gravy
1 can (8 ounces) stewed tomatoes, undrained
3/4 teaspoon dried thyme
1/8 teaspoon pepper
1 package (16 ounces) frozen vegetable mixture (with potato)

Combine gravy, tomatoes, 3/4 cup water, thyme and pepper in large saucepan; bring to a boil. Stir in meatballs and vegetable mixture. Reduce heat. Cook 10 to 15 minutes or until meatballs are heated through, stirring occasionally.

National Cattleman's Beef Association   www.beefitswhatsfordinner.com

Mexican Bake

Serves 4

    1 can tamales, sliced
    1 can Mexicorn, drained
    1 can red kidney beans, drained
    $1/2$ to 1 cup cheese, grated

Preheat oven to 350 degrees. Layer tamales in bottom of casserole. Top with corn, then beans. Sprinkle cheese over all and bake 30 minutes.

Laurie Giauque   Olympus High School, Salt Lake City, UT

Mexican Mix-Up

Serves 4

    1 (15 ounce) can tamales, cut up
    1 (15 ounce) can chili, with beans
    1 (15 ounce) can whole kernel corn
    1 (15 once) can diced tomatoes
    $1/2$ bag corn chips
    1 cup cheddar cheese, shredded

Put first 4 ingredients in medium saucepan and simmer, uncovered, for 15 to 20 minutes. Serve in bowls topped with corn chips and shredded cheese.

"This is the best! And you can keep the ingredients on hand
for those emergency quick dinners."

Penny Niadna   Golden West High School, Visalia, CA

Navajo Tacos

Serves 8

    20 frozen rolls, thawed
    6 cups chili
    2 cups cheddar cheese, shredded
    Shredded lettuce
    Green onions, sliced
    Diced tomatoes
    Picante sauce or salsa
    Sour cream, optional

Thaw rolls, but do not allow to rise. Heat chili and place in a 9" x 13" pan. Cut each thawed frozen roll into fourths. Place rolls on top of chili. Sprinkle with cheese. Bake at 350 degrees for 25 to 30 minutes. To serve, shred lettuce and place on individual plates. Top with sliced green onions, and diced tomatoes. Place a generous serving of chili and bread on top of lettuce. Top with salsa and a dollop of sour cream.

"Recipe may easily be cut in half and baked in a 9" x 9" square
an for smaller families."

Jennifer Hill   Kearns High School, Kearns , Utah

One Skillet Spaghetti

Serves 6

$1/2$ pound hamburger
1 (medium) onion, chopped (about $1/2$ cup)
2 cups whole tomatoes, undrained
$1/4$ cup green pepper, chopped
$1/4$ cup water
1 teaspoon salt
$1/2$ teaspoon sugar
$1/2$ teaspoon chili powder
3 $1/2$ ounces thin spaghetti, uncooked
$1/2$ cup cheddar cheese, shredded

Cook and stir hamburger with onion in a 10" skillet or Dutch oven until hamburger is light brown; drain off excess grease. Stir in tomatoes, with liquid, green pepper, water, salt, sugar, chili powder and spaghetti, breaking up tomatoes with fork. Heat to boiling; reduce heat. Cover and simmer, stirring occasionally until spaghetti is tender, about 30 minutes. (Add a little water during cooking if necessary.) Sprinkle with cheese; cover and heat until cheese melts.

"My students loved this recipe–it is actually like a chili."

Janice Tuttle   Mills High School, Millbrae, CA

Pot Roast Made Easy

Serves 4-6

3 pound roast
1 pacakge brown gravy mix
1 package Ranch dressing mix
1 package Italian dressing mix
1 cup water
$1/2$ onion, chopped
2 to 3 potatoes, cut in quarters

Using a crockpot, add roast, packaged mixes, water and onion. Cook on low for 6 to 8 hours. Three hours before serving, add the potatoes and continue cooking. Serve with veggies and salad and you have a meal.

"Start this in the morning, have your kids add the potatoes when they get home from school and by 6 pm you have a meal ready to go. The crockpot makes the meat tender and juicy, while the mixes make an excellent gravy. Enjoy!"

Mary Nafis   Montclair High School, Montclair, CA

Pot Roast Plus
Serves 3 - 4

2 $1/2$ to 3 pounds Harris Ranch Homestyle
   Beef Pot Roast, fully cooked
1 package McCormick Brown Gravy mix, dry
$3/4$ cup red wine
1 tablespoon cornstarch
1 package baby carrots
8 to 10 (small) red potatoes

Preheat oven to 350 degrees. Open pot roast package and place in a 9" x 13" roasting pan. Pour some liquid from package into a 2 cup (or more) measuring cup. Add dry gravy mix, red wine and cornstarch and mix well. Place carrots and potatoes around roast in pan and pour gravy mixture over everything. Cover with foil and bake 45 minutes to 1 hour.

"So easy, quick and a favorite!"

Gail McAuley   Lincoln High School, Stockton, CA

Potato Boats
Serves 6

1 pound hamburger meat
3 cans Franco Chicken gravy
salt and pepper, to taste
mashed potatoes, prepared

Brown and drain the meat. Add the gravy to the meat. Season with salt and pepper to taste. Serve the meat mixture on top of the mashed potatoes.

"I use home made mashed potatoes, but boxed dried potato flakes work well too."

Mary Mondientz   Buchanan High School, Clovis, CA

Quick Protein Wraps
Serves 4

4 (large) whole wheat tortillas
6 to 8 ounces leftover steak or chicken, sliced
1 (small) can ranch style beans
6 ounces cheese, cheddar or pepper jack, grated
1 (medium) tomato, diced and seeded
3 green onions, diced
2 cups lettuce, shredded
sour cream and taco sauce for garnish

Heat the beans in a sauce pan. Place a tortilla in a large, dry skillet. Spread $1/4$ of the cheese on the tortilla and apply heat to the pan. Next, spread $1/4$ of the meat. Heat the tortilla just until the cheese has melted. Slide out onto plate. Top with some beans, tomatoes, and lettuce. Garnish with sauces inside if desired. Roll up and slice in half, on the bias. Serve with extra beans and fruit for a balanced meal.

"These wraps are so delicious and allow you to use up leftovers as well as allowing your family to prepare each wrap to suit their personal tastes. My family enjoys the steak cold so it doesn't become overcooked by reheating. But you can heat it ahead of time if you desire."

Delaine Smith   West Valley High School, Cottonwood, CA

Quick Sloppy Joes
Serves 4

1 1/2 pounds ground beef
1/2 cup onion, diced
1/2 teaspoon salt
1/8 teaspoon pepper
1 (8 ounce) can condensed chicken gumbo soup
3 tablespoons catsup
2 teaspoons prepared mustard
rolls, cooked pasta or cooked rice
4 slices cheese

Brown ground meat over medium heat; drain. Stir in onion, salt, pepper, soup, catsup and mustard. Cover and simmer 20 minutes. Remove lid and simmer until desired thickness. Serve on rolls, pasta or rice, with cheese.

"Quick, easy, and my students love it!"

Dale Sheehan   Santana High School, Santee, CA

Real Philly Cheese Steak Sandwich
Serves 4

2 tablespoons extra-virgin olive oil
1 (large) sweet onion, peeled, halved, sliced into
   paper thin half moon wedges
4 bell peppers, halved, seeded and sliced into thick wedges
salt and pepper, to taste
water, to moisten
1 pound steak (sirloin, rib eye, eye of chuck) frozen,
   cut into very thin slices
1 jar Cheez Whiz or sharp provolone or mozzarella
4 Amorosos rolls or French or hoagie rolls

Warm oil in large skillet over low heat heat; add onions and cook 8 to 10 minutes, until caramelized and softened, stirring frequently. Do not allow them to brown. Transfer onions to a bowl; add pepper to same skillet and stir over low heat. Cook 10 to 15 minutes, until soft and tender, flipping often. Transfer to bowl with onions. Season with salt and pepper to taste and cover to keep warm. In a clean skillet, moisten steak and cook over medium heat. Cook in two batches, until lightly browned and cooked through, stirring often. Just before steak is done, top with cheese. As soon as cheese melts, put mixture on rolls, then top with onion/pepper mixture.

Dave Rieck   Las Plumas High School, Oroville, CA

Rice-A-Roni Meatballs

Serves 4

>   1 box Beef Rice-A-Roni
>   1 pound ground beef
>   2 slices bread, dampened, torn into small pieces
>   1 egg
>   1/4 teaspoon garlic salt
>   1/8 teaspoon pepper
>   2 1/2 cups water
>   oil, for frying

Place Rice-A-Roni in bowl. Add ground beef, torn bread, egg, garlic salt and pepper. Mix with hands and form into balls. Heat oil in skillet; brown meatballs carefully turning with fork. Sprinkle with seasoning packet and add water. Cover and lower heat to simmer 20 minutes. Check meat and turn to keep from sticking. Sauce will be gravy upon cooling.

"A great, quick, easy main dish for the family on the go!"

Sonja Tyree   Ayala High School, Chino Hills, CA

Skillet Meal

Serves 6

>   12 ounces macaroni, dry
>   1 pound ground beef
>   1 (medium) onion, chopped
>   1 (16 ounce) can diced tomatoes with green chiles
>   2 (8 ounce) cans tomato sauce
>   1 can corn, drained
>   1 to 2 cups cheese, shredded

Cook macaroni and drain. Brown hamburger with onion while macaroni cooks. Add drained macaroni to browned meat mixture. Add tomatoes, tomato sauce and corn; mix well. Top with cheese, cover with lid. Cook over medium-low heat until heated through and cheese melts.

"A quick meal for those 'what should we have for dinner' nights.
Amounts can be altered to your preferences or what you have on hand."

Celeste Giron   Riverton High School, Riverton, UT

Spanish Rice Dish

Serves 6

1 pound ground beef
1 package Lipton Spanish Rice
1 (15 ounce) can stewed tomatoes, drained (reserve juice)
1 (15 ounce) can olives, sliced
1 cup canned or frozen corn

Sauté ground beef until pink is gone; drain. Prepare Spanish rice according to package directions. (Use the reserved tomato juice to make up the 1 cup of liquid for rice.) While rice is cooking, add the drained ground beef, tomatoes, sliced olives and corn. Cook until rice is tender.

"This recipe is so fast and good. Always a favorite for my family."

Dian Abbott   Corcoran High School, Corcoran, CA

String Cheese Manicotti

Serves 6 - 8

1 package manicotti shells
1 pound ground beef
1 onion, chopped
1 green bell pepper, chopped
1 clove garlic minced
1 jar spaghetti sauce
14 pieces string cheese
1 $1/2$ cups mozzarella cheese, shredded

Cook manicotti according to package directions; set aside. Preheat oven to 350 degrees. In a large skillet, sauté ground beef with onion, green pepper and garlic; cook until no longer pink and drain excess liquid. Stir in spaghetti sauce. Spread half of the meat mixture into a greased 9" x 13" pan. Stuff each shell with a piece of string cheese. Place over meat sauce and top with remaining sauce. Sprinkle with mozzarella cheese and bake 25 to 30 minutes.

Karen Tilson   Poly High School, Riverside, CA

Stroganoff Sandwiches
Serves 6

1 pound ground beef
$1/4$ cup green onion, chopped
1 cup sour cream
1 teaspoon Worcestershire sauce
$1/8$ teaspoon garlic powder
$3/4$ teaspoon salt
1 loaf French bread, unsliced
butter or margarine, softened
2 tomatoes, sliced
1 green pepper, cut into rings
1 cup American cheese, shredded

In a skillet, cook meat and onion until meat is browned; drain. Stir in sour cream, Worcestershire sauce, garlic powder and salt; heat through - do not boil. Meanwhile, cut bread in half lengthwise. Place halves, cut side up, on baking sheet. Broil 4" to 5" from heat for 2 to 3 minutes or until toasted. Spread lightly with butter or margarine. Spread hot meat mixture on toasted bread. Top with slices of tomato, green pepper and grated cheese. Broil 2 minutes longer. Slice to make 6 servings.

"Serve with a green salad for a quick winter meal."

Kris Hawkins   Clovis West High School, Fresno, CA

Stuffed Green Peppers
Serves 4

4 (large) green or red peppers
$1/4$ cup water
1 pound lean ground beef
1 (medium) onion, finely chopped
1 clove garlic, minced
1 teaspoon salt
$1/4$ teaspoon pepper
1 $1/2$ cups rice, cooked
1 tablespoon fresh parsley, minced
1 (8 ounce) can tomato sauce, divided

Wash peppers, remove tops and seeds. Place upright in 2 quart micro-proof casserole. Pour water over bottom of dish and cook, covered, on high for 2 minutes. Drain water. Let peppers stand while preparing filling. Crumble beef into glass mixing bowl. Add onion and cook on high 4 minutes, or until meat loses its color, stirring once during cooking. Drain fat. Stir in garlic, salt, pepper, rice, parsley, and $1/2$ cup tomato sauce. Fill peppers with mixture, mounding on top. Replace peppers in casserole and top each with remaining tomato sauce. Cook, covered, on high 10 to 12 minutes, or until peppers are tender.

"My kids love this. It's quick and easy to make! Cook the meat in a skillet too."
Debra Warren   **Hueneme High School, Oxnard, CA**

Taco Potatoes
Serves 4 - 6

4 to 6 potatoes, baked
1 pound hamburger
1 package taco seasoning mix
Toppings: Sour cream, shredded cheese, chopped tomatoes, sliced jalapeños

Bake potatoes in oven or microwave. Meanwhile, prepare hamburger with taco seasoning according to package directions. Split potatoes down center and fill with cooked hamburger mixture. Top as desired.

"My students love these after they try them.
At first they are skeptical about the potatoes!"
Sheri Rader   **Chaparral High School, Las Vegas, NV**

Teriyaki Beef Bowl
Serves 4

2 cups short grain rice (will yield 6 cups cooked rice)
$1/4$ cup soy sauce
3 tablespoons sugar
1 tablespoon mirin or sake (rice wine)
$1/2$ teaspoon fresh ginger, grated
$1/2$ teaspoon fresh garlic, minced
1 pound rib eye steak, thinly sliced

Cook rice according to package directions. In a small bowl, mix together soy sauce, sugar, mirin or sake, ginger and garlic. Heat skillet. Pan fry thinly sliced steak about 1 minute on each side. Pour soy sauce mixture over meat and continue frying for 1 more minute. Divide rice into bowls. Top with meat mixture.

"Quick, easy and delicious. Thinly sliced rib eye steak (sukiyaki style)
can be purchased at Asian markets."
Reiko Ikkanda   **South Pasadena Middle School, South Pasadena, CA**

Western Casserole

Serves 6

1 pound ground beef
1 (medium) onion, chopped
1 (16 ounce) bottle barbecue sauce
$1/_2$ cup molasses
1 (28 ounce) can pork 'n beans
1 can Pillsbury biscuits
$1/_2$ pound cheddar cheese, grated

Brown ground beef and drain excess fat. Add chopped onions. Stir in barbecue sauce and molasses. Add the beans; mix well. Pour into casserole dish. Cut biscuits into quarters and place on top of casserole mixture. Bake at 350 degrees for 25 minutes. Remove from oven and spread grated cheese on top. Bake 5 minutes more, or until cheese melts.

"This is a recipe that one of my students shared with me many years ago, and my family has really enjoyed it."

Pat Smith   Kern Valley High School, Lake Isabella, CA

Main Dishes with Poultry

2-Step Chicken Broccoli Divan
Serves 4 - 5

1 pound fresh broccoli, cut into spears
   or 1 (10 ounce) package frozen broccoli spears, cooked; drained
1 $^1/_2$ cups cooked chicken, diced
1 can cream of broccoli soup
$^1/_3$ cup milk
$^1/_2$ cup cheddar cheese, shredded
2 tablespoons dry bread crumbs
1 tablespoon butter, melted

In a shallow casserole dish, arrange broccoli spears on bottom. Top with chicken. Combine soup and milk; pour over chicken. Sprinkle with cheese. Toast bread crumbs in melted butter and sprinkle over cheese. Bake in conventional oven at 450 degrees for 15 minutes or cook in microwave on high for 6 minutes. Cover with waxed paper and rotate dish after 3 minutes cooking in microwave.

"This is great recipe to serve over rice or noodles."

Laurie Owen   Challenger Middle School, San Diego, CA

Almost California Pizza Kitchen BBQ Chicken Pizza
Serves 4

1 Boboli pizza crust
1 package grilled chicken breast strips
1 cup favorite BBQ sauce
2 ounces gouda cheese, shredded
4 ounces mozzarella cheese, shredded
$^1/_2$ red onion, thinly sliced
2 tablespoons fresh cilantro, chopped

Preheat oven to 450 degrees. Place Boboli on baking pan. Cut chicken into bite-size pieces. Mix with 2 tablespoons of the BBQ sauce in a small mixing bowl. Coat the crust generously with the remaining BBQ sauce. Sprinkle smoked gouda cheese over sauce. Cover with most of the mozzarella cheese.

74

Top with chicken pieces. Cover with the thinly sliced red onion. Top with remaining mozzarella cheese. Bake for 10-12 minutes until cheese is melted. Remove from oven and top with cilantro. Slice and serve!

"This is an attempt to duplicate one of my favorite pizzas at home. It is so quick and I usually keep the ingredients on hand, when I need to have something ready in a hurry."

Julie Shelburne   Tulare Union High School, Tulare, CA

Baked Chicken & Rice Casserole

Serves 4

1 $1/_2$ teaspoons apple cider vinegar
1 teaspoon salt
$1/_2$ teaspoon pepper
$1/_2$ teaspoon paprika
1 (1.5 ounce) package onion soup mix, divided
$1/_4$ cup margarine
8 pieces chicken
1 (10.75 ounce) can condensed cream of mushroom soup, undiluted
2 $1/_4$ cups Minute or original or premium rice, uncooked

Preheat oven to 350 degrees. Mix vinegar, salt, pepper, paprika and 1 teaspoon onion soup mix in small bowl. Sprinkle over chicken pieces. Melt margarine in large skillet and add chicken, browning on both sides; set aside. Place condensed soup in 4 cup measuring cup. Add water to make 3 cups. Stir in remaining onion soup mix. Place rice, chicken and 1 $1/_3$ cups soup mixture in bottom of a 3 quart baking dish. Pour remaining 1 $1/_2$ cups soup mixture over chicken and cover. Bake 1 hour or until chicken is done.

Darlene V. Sears Brown   Golden Valley Middle School, San Bernardino, CA

Baked Chicken Supreme

Serves 6

1 clove garlic, pressed
1 $1/_2$ cups sour cream
2 tablespoons lemon juice
1 $1/_2$ teaspoons seasoned salt
1 teaspoon paprika
dash hot sauce
3 pounds chicken pieces (boneless, skinless, if desired)
1 $1/_2$ cups herb seasoned dressing mix, finely crushed
1 cube butter or margarine, melted

Place first six ingredients in large zipper-type plastic bag; mix well. Add chicken pieces and marinate overnight. Remove chicken. Roll each piece in crumbs and place in large oblong baking dish. Drizzle with melted butter or margarine. Bake at 350 degrees until chicken is tender and golden brown, about 1 hour.

"I like to serve this with simple low-calorie side dishes, such as steamed broccoli or green beans and broiled or fresh sliced tomatoes."

Winn Yablonski   John F. Kennedy High School, La Palma, CA

Can Opener Chicken Enchilada
Serves 6

1 (10.75 ounce) can cream of chicken soup
1 (8 ounce) can creamed corn
$1/2$ cup green onions, chopped
3 tablespoons taco seasoning
2 (5 ounce) cans premium chunked chicken
$1/2$ cup sour cream
$1/4$ cup milk
1 $1/2$ cups cheddar cheese, shredded, divided
$1/2$ cup black olives, sliced
12 (6 inch) tortillas

Preheat oven to 350 degrees. Mix the first 8 ingredients together using only half of the cheese. Spread $1/2$ cup of mixture in each tortilla; roll and place in a 11" x 7" baking dish. Repeat until all tortillas are filled. Pour remaining mixture on top of tortillas and top with the remaining cheese and olives. Bake 15 to 20 minutes until thoroughly heated and cheese is bubbly. Allow to sit 5 minutes before serving.

"This is a fast and simple recipe because most of the ingredients come from a can!"

Jennifer Hill   Kearns High School, Kearns, UT

Cheddar Chicken Pot Pie
Serves 4 - 6

1 cup cooked diced chicken
1 cup frozen broccoli (or vegetable of your choice)
1 (15 ounce) can cream of mushroom soup
1 (9") pie shell, frozen
1 cup sharp cheddar cheese, shredded

Preheat oven to 375 degrees. Gently combine chicken, vegetables and soup in medium bowl. Pour mixture into pie shell. Sprinkle cheese on top. Bake 45 to 60 minutes, until cheese is melted and mixture is bubbly.

Diane Wolak   Martin Luther King High School, Riverside, CA

Chicken & Garlic Pasta

Serves 6

4 boneless skinless chicken breasts
1 pound angel hair pasta
1/2 cup butter
2 tablespoons garlic
fresh basil, chopped (optional)

Cut chicken into bite-sized pieces and saute in a skillet over medium heat. While chicken is cooking, boil water for noodles. Cook noodles al dente, drain, then add butter and garlic. Toss cooked chicken with pasta and serve. Sprinkle with basil, if desired.

"This is simple, fast, and good."

Christina Sargent   Delano High School, Delano, Ca

Chicken Broccoli Bake

Serves 6

1 box stuffing mix, reconstituted but not baked
1 can cream of chicken soup
1/3 cup milk
6 chicken breasts, or 10 to 12 chicken tenders
1 small bag frozen broccoli
2 1/2 cups grated cheddar

Preheat oven to 375 degrees. Prepare stuffing according to box but without baking; set aside. Combine cream of chicken soup and milk; set aside. Layer in 9" x 13" baking dish the chicken, frozen broccoli, cream soup mixture, cheese and top with reconstituted stuffing mix. Cover with aluminum foil and bake 30 to 35 minutes or until chicken is done. Note: Frozen chicken may be used but increases baking time. For a crunchier stuffing, take aluminum foil off the last 10 minutes of baking.

"This recipe can be assembled in the morning, refrigerated,
and baked at dinner time. Leftovers freeze well also."

Shauna Robinson   Centennial High School, Las Vegas, NV

Chicken Curry
Serves 2 - 4

2 cups hot steamed rice
2 (small) or 1 (large) onion, diced
$1/2$ cube margarine or butter
1 $1/2$ boneless, skinless chicken breasts, cut $1/2$" x 2"
salt and pepper, to taste
1 can cream of mushroom soup
$1/4$ to $1/2$ teaspoon chili powder
$1/2$ to 1 teaspoon curry powder
$1/2$ cup cashews, salted, chopped (optional)

Prepare rice according to package directions. Sauté onions in melted butter over low heat until transparent. Add chicken and cook thoroughly (no pink centers). Salt and pepper to taste as you are cooking. Add mushroom soup, chili powder and curry powder. Heat completely, blending seasonings thoroughly as you stir. Serve over hot, steamed rice. Top with cashews if desired.

Donna Ward   Bella Vista High School, Fairoaks, CA

Chicken Florentine
Serves 4

4 chicken breasts, pounded thin
salt and pepper, to taste
2 tablespoons flour
2 to 4 tablespoons oil
3 cups spinach
water, to boil
4 slices Swiss cheese
juice of 1 lemon

Preheat oven to 375 degrees. Pound chicken breasts and season to taste. Dredge lightly in flour. Heat oil and brown on both sides of chicken. Bring water to boil and cook spinach until it turns bright green - do not overcook! Drain well. In a foil-lined baking pan, place chicken breasts in a single layer. Top each with spinach and a slice of cheese. Squeeze lemon juice over chicken and bake 10 to 20 minutes, until cheese bubbles.

*"This is also fabulous with sautéed mushrooms in
addition to the spinach and cheese."*

Alicia Pucci   Kenilworth Junior High School, Petaluma, CA

Chicken Parmigiana With Pasta

Serves 4

4 Banquet chicken patties
   or 1 box Morningstar Farms Chik Patties for meatless
cooking spray
8 oz. ($^{1}/_{2}$ package) penne, spaghetti, or any pasta
$^{1}/_{2}$ of a 26 ounce jar Ragu spaghetti sauce
Parmesan cheese, grated
parsley for garnish

Preheat oven for chicken patties according to package directions. Bring water to boil in large pot for pasta. Place frozen chicken patties on foil-lined cookie sheet. Spray patties with cooking spray. Bake according to package directions. Cook pasta according to package directions. While pasta is cooking, heat spaghetti sauce. Stir about 1 cup spaghetti sauce into drained pasta. Place pasta mixture on a large platter or individual pasta bowls and top with chicken patties; ladle remaining spaghetti sauce over each patty. Top with cheese and chopped parsley. Keep warm until ready to serve.

"Serve with a salad and garlic bread. Nice enough for company
with Lemon (No-bake) Cheesecake for dessert."

Sharlene Young   Ysmael Villegas Middle School, Riverside, CA

Chicken Pie

Serves 6 - 8

1 can chicken soup
1 cup milk
2 cups cooked chicken
2 cups frozen corn and peas
2 unbaked pie shells

Preheat oven to 350 degrees. Combine first 4 ingredients and divide mixture between both unbaked pie shells. Bake 50 minutes.

"This is so fast and easy to put together after a long day at work.
It is one of my family's favorites."

Debbie Farr   Foothill High School, Santa Ana, CA

Chicken Pita Wrap

Serves 4 - 5

1 chicken breast
2 tablespoons Italian marinade
1 teaspoon butter
4 to 5 pieces Pita or flat bread
lettuce, shredded
tomato, sliced
onion, sliced
2 to 3 teaspoons Ranch dressing

Slice chicken breast into long strips. Cook on medium heat in a large frying pan. After chicken is fully cooked (no longer pink and juices run clear), add marinade and cook about 5 minutes more. Add butter to a small pan on medium heat and toast pita or flat bread on both sides until crisp. Add half of the chicken breast to open side of pita or flat bread. Add lettuce, tomato and onion and top with Ranch dressing. Fold together and serve.

Kelly Smith   **Las Vegas High School, Las Vegas, NV**

Chicken Pockets

Serves 4

1 (8 ounce) package cream cheese
2 cups chicken, cooked, diced
$1/4$ cup margarine
4 to 6 green onions, chopped
1 (small) can mushrooms, drained, chopped
salt and pepper, to taste
2 packages crescent rolls
seasoned bread crumbs
chopped nuts
1 can cream of chicken soup
$1/2$ cup milk

Preheat oven to 350 degrees. Mix cream cheese with chicken, margarine, green onion and mushrooms; salt and pepper to taste. Unroll crescent rolls. Put a rounded spoonful of chicken mixture on large end of each roll. Roll up and dip in melted butter, then roll in seasoned bread crumbs and chopped nuts. Place on baking pan and bake 20 minutes. While chicken pockets are baking, heat soup with milk. When ready to serve, place sauce in pitcher and serve with hot pockets.

Rebecca Hutchings   **Spring Valley High School, Las Vegas, NV**

Chicken Quesadillas

Serves 4

1 frozen chicken breast
8 flour tortillas
$1/4$ cup onion, finely diced
$1/4$ bell pepper, finely diced
1 cup cheddar and mozzarella cheese, grated

Preheat oven to 425 degrees. Place chicken on a microwave safe plate. Cover loosely with plastic wrap and microwave 2 minutes at 30% power. Remove from microwave and cut into small cubes. Recover and microwave 2 minutes on high. Remove, stir, and cook in 1 minute increments until done. Drain in a colander. Place 4 tortillas on a cookie sheet. Sprinkle diced onion and diced green pepper evenly over all tortillas. Sprinkle cubed chicken evenly over all tortillas. Divide the shredded cheese evenly among all tortillas. Top with remaining tortillas. Bake 8 to 10 minutes. Cool slightly and cut into pie shaped slices. Serve.

"Add a salad to this and a quick dinner is ready in just a few minutes!"
Barbara Henshaw   Foothill High School, Pleasanton, CA

Chicken Roll-ups

Serves 4

2 to 3 chicken breasts, boiled and diced (or 1 can canned chicken)
4 ounces cream cheese
1 (4 ounce) can mushrooms (optional)
$1/4$ teaspoon salt
$1/4$ teaspoon pepper
1 package crescent rolls
2 tablespoons butter or margarine
$1/2$ cup bread crumbs
$1/2$ cup Parmesan cheese, grated
1 package of chicken gravy, prepared or 1 can cream of chicken soup

Preheat oven to 375 degrees. Mix together chicken, cream cheese, mushrooms, and salt and pepper. Roll into 8 equal balls. Open 1 package crescent rolls, place 1 chicken ball in the center of each individual roll. Roll up as directed on package. Roll in melted butter, then in mixture of bread crumbs and Parmesan cheese. Bake 10 to 15 minutes or until browned. Serve with chicken gravy or warmed cream of chicken soup.

"Always seem to hit the spot."
Linda A. Stokes   Riverton High School, Riverton, UT

Chicken Salad Melts

Serves 4

>   1 1/2 cups cooked chicken, finely chopped
>   1/2 cup mayonnaise
>   4 ounces processed Velveeta cheese, cubed
>   2 tablespoons each green pepper, onion and ripe olives, chopped
>   2 tablespoons sweet pickle relish
>   4 sandwich rolls

In a bowl, combine chicken with mayonnaise, cheese, green pepper, onion, olives and relish. Split rolls in half. Place cut side up on greased baking sheet. Spoon about 1/4 cup chicken salad on each roll half. Broil 4" from heat for 5 to 6 minutes or until cheese is melted.

"Great for leftover chicken. Delicious, satisfying and inexpensive. Julie Swallows gave me this recipe from a magazine."

Darlene V. Sears Brown   Golden Valley Middle School, San Bernardino, CA

Chicken Scaloppini with Lemon & Capers

Serves 2 - 4

>   4 boneless, skinless chicken breasts, (about 5 ounces each)
>   1/2 teaspoon salt
>   1/8 teaspoon pepper
>   2 tablespoons butter
>   1 tablespoon olive oil
>   1/3 cup dry white wine
>   1/3 cup reduced sodium chicken broth
>   3 tablespoons lemon juice
>   2 tablespoons capers, rinsed and drained
>   2 tablespoons parsley, finely chopped

Pound chicken to 1/4" thickness between sheets of waxed paper or plastic wrap. Season with salt and pepper. In large frying pan, melt butter with olive oil over medium heat. Add chicken and cook 2 minutes. Turn and cook 2 minutes longer, or until white throughout. Remove to a warmed platter; cover loosely with foil to keep warm. Pour wine into pan. Add stock and boil until reduced by half, about 2 minutes. Add lemon juice, capers and parsley. Pour over chicken and serve immediately.

"Don't try to do a quick sauté like this for more than 4 people. It's too much to do at the last minute and should be eaten as soon as it's cooked."

Mary Coffman   Reed High School, Sparks, NV

Chicken Tacos

Serves 8-10 servings

1 whole chicken or 2 whole chicken breasts
1 can green enchilada sauce orTrader Joe's green chile sauce
Toppings: Shredded cheese, shredded lettuce,
    chopped tomatoes, chopped onions, cilantro

Put chicken in crockpot. Pour sauce over chicken. Turn on high and all day. Remove meat from bones and shred. Place chicken in warmed tortillas and top as desired.

"This could be done with pork."

Carole Call   Costa Mesa High School, Costa Mesa , CA

Chicken, Tuna or Turkey Casserole

Serves 6

1 can cream of mushroom soup
1 cup milk
1 cup mayonnaise
1 cup cheese, shredded
1 teaspoon curry (optional)
1 can tuna or leftover chicken or turkey
$1/2$ package corkscrew pasta, cooked
Toppings: Cheese, bread crumbs or dressing

Combine all ingredients and pour into casserole dish. Bake at 350 degrees for 20 minutes or microwave on high 10 minutes, until heated through.

"This is best used with leftover turkey and then topped with leftover dressing."

Karyn Hobbs   Lemoore High School, Lemoore, CA

Chicken Vegetable Stir Fry

Serves 4

Brown or white rice (brown is healthier)
2 tablespoons olive oil
2 skinless, boneless chicken breasts cut in strips
$1/2$ onion sliced
1 to 2 teaspoons ginger root minced
$1/2$ cup carrots sliced
$1/2$ cup green, yellow, and/or red bell pepper sliced
$3/4$ cup broccoli chopped
2 tablespoons teriyaki sauce
$1/4$ cup bean sprouts

Put rice on to cook, following instructions on package. Add oil to frying pan or wok and heat to medium-high. Add chicken and cook 2 minutes, stirring constantly. Add onions and ginger and cook for 2 minutes, then add carrots, bell peppers, and broccoli and teriyaki sauce. Continue stirring and cook for 2 to 3 minutes until vegetables are tender crisp. Add sprouts last and cook for 1 minute. Serve over rice.

"This is a healthy quick one pan meal. You can substitute fish or meat for the chicken, and substitute your favorite vegetables."

Linda Johnson   Johansen High School, Modesto, CA

Coconut Curry Chicken
Serves 4

4 boneless, skinless chicken breasts
3 tablespoons butter, melted
1 cup dried coconut, shredded
2 teaspoons curry powder
salt, to taste
chutney or fruit salsa

Preheat oven to 350 degrees. Rinse chicken and pat dry. Pour butter into a 9" x 13" baking dish. In a pie plate, combine coconut and curry powder. Dip chicken in butter to coat, then roll in coconut. Place chicken pieces slightly apart in the baking dish. Pat any remaining coconut mixture on top. Sprinkle with salt. Bake 20 to 25 minutes, until chicken is no longer pink in center of thickest part (cut to test). Serve with chutney or fruit salsa.

"This unique recipe was a real hit with my family. Even the picky eaters loved it!"

Pam Ford   Temecula Valley High School, Temecula, CA

Crispy Chicken Nuggets
Makes 2 - 3 dozen

4 boneless chicken breasts
1 (5.5 ounce) package barbecued potato chips, finely crushed
$1/4$ teaspoon paprika
dash pepper
$1/4$ cup milk

Preheat oven to 400 degrees. Cut each breast half into 6 or 8 chunks, about 1 $1/2$ inches square. Combine potato chips, paprika and pepper. Dip chicken chunks in milk. Roll in potato chip mixture. Place in single layer on baking sheet. Bake 10 minutes.

"Disappear immediately at our classroom appetizer buffet!"

Carolyn Frohlich   Sequoia High School, Redwood City, CA

Crockpot Chicken

Serves 4-6

4 to 6 chicken breasts, frozen
20 to 24 ounces (approximately) of your favorite
   BBQ sauce, salsa, or salad dressing

Place frozen chicken in a crockpot. Pour your favorite sauce over the top, cover and cook on low all day.

"Can't get any easier!"

Marilyn Bankhead   San Marcos High School, San Marcos, CA

Crunchy Ranch Chicken

Serves 4

1 cup corn flakes, crushed
1 cup Parmesan cheese, shredded
1 packet ranch salad dressing mix
imitation butter spray
4 boneless skinless chicken breasts

Preheat oven to 350 degrees. Combine corn flakes, Parmesan cheese, and ranch dressing mix in bowl. Spray each chicken breast with imitation butter spray and dip in corn flake mixture. Place on cookie sheet and sprinkle remaining mixture on top. Bake uncovered, 45 minutes.

"Thanks to Darin Petzold and Dionne Bargabus for sharing this quick and healthy recipe!"

Rhonda Nelson   Rancho Santa Margarita Intermediate School, RSM, CA

Easy Chicken Parmigiana

Serves 6

4 cups prepared spaghetti sauce
6 chicken breasts, breaded, frozen
6 slices mozzarella cheese

Preheat oven to 350 degrees. In a 9" x 9" glass pan, place 1 cup sauce. Place frozen chicken patties on top and pour remaining sauce over top. Place a slice of cheese on each patty. Bake 30 minutes or until chicken is hot and cheese has melted.

"Serve this with garlic bread and salad!"

Debi Weiss   Ayala High School, Chino Hills, CA

Fast Chinese Chicken Noodles

Serves 4-5

 $1/2$ pound spaghetti noodles
 1 (10 ounce) package frozen vegetables mix;
   with broccoli, carrots, cauliflower, etc.
 $1/4$ head cabbage, chopped
 2 chicken breasts, cooked, cut up
 $1/2$ to 1 cup Yoshida's Gourmet Sauce

Boil spaghetti according to package directions. Meanwhile, cook frozen vegetables in the microwave. Add cabbage to vegetables and cook about 1 to 2 additional minutes. Drain spaghetti; add vegetables, chicken and sauce. Heat through and serve.

"This is a great imitation of oriental noodle dishes with most items on hand. Add other vegetables to suit your taste."

Pamela Bonilla   Valley View High School, Moreno Valley, CA

Feta Chicken

Serves 4

 1 cup plain yogurt
 1 (large) clove garlic, minced
 $1/2$ teaspoon dried oregano
 $1/4$ teaspoon pepper
 4 boneless, skinless chicken breasts
 $1/3$ cup feta cheese

Mix together yogurt, garlic, oregano and pepper in a ziploc bag. Add chicken to bag and marinate 30 minutes. Remove chicken and broil approximately 6 minutes on one side. Turn chicken and baste second side with yogurt marinade. Discard remaining marinade. Top with crumbled feta cheese and cook for an additional 4 minutes or until chicken is cooked through.

Tisha Ludeman   Brookhurst Junior High School, Anaheim, CA

Garlic Chicken Pasta

Serves 6

 1 package pasta
 $1/4$ cup olive oil
 2 tablespoons garlic, chopped
 $1/2$ cup fresh basil, chopped
 2 packages precooked grilled chicken strips
 Parmesan cheese, to taste

Bring water to a boil and cook your choice of pasta according to package directions. While pasta is cooking, heat oil in a large frying pan. Sauté garlic until soft, about 1 to 2 minutes. When pasta is done, drain and return to cooking pot. Stir in oil and garlic mixture; add basil. Place pasta on plate; top with chicken strips and serve. Pass Parmesan cheese separately at the table.

"This recipe was developed out of necessity.
I had fresh basil and chicken on hand; it goes well with cooked pasta."

Beth Guerrero   Selma High School, Selma, CA

Green Chile Chicken Enchiladas
Serves 6

    12 corn tortillas
    2 cans cream of chicken soup
    1 cup sour cream
    1 cup chicken or turkey, cooked, diced
    1 can green chiles, diced
    1 cup cheddar cheese, shredded

Preheat oven to 375 degrees. Mix 1 can of the soup with sour cream, chiles and chicken. Warm the tortillas (works in the microwave). Fill each tortilla with some of the mixture, roll up and place seam side down in a 9" x 13" baking dish. Mix the remaining can of soup with remaining filling and place on top. Sprinkle with cheese and bake about 20 to 30 minutes, until heated through and cheese is melted.

"May be made and frozen ahead of time very easily. Use whatever size
can of chiles you like. Mixed cheddar and jack cheese works well too."

Peg Ellington   Yucca Valley High School, Yucca Valley, CA

Honey Baked Chicken
Serves 4

    1/4 cup margarine
    1/2 cup honey
    1 tablespoon Dijon mustard
    1 teaspoon salt
    1 teaspoon curry powder
    4 boneless, skinless chicken breasts

Preheat oven to 375 degrees, Place margarine in a 9" square pan in oven to melt for about 5 minutes. Stir honey, mustard, salt and curry powder into melted margarine. Coat both sides of chicken pieces with mixture as you place it in the pan. Bake 20 minutes, turn and bake 15 minutes more. Serve with rice or noodles.

"Add a salad and you have a great, quick dinner."

Jane Reed   Dublin High School, Dublin, CA

Honey Nut Chicken

Serves 4

4 ounces ($2/3$ cup) honey roasted peanuts
$1/2$ cup plain bread crumbs
1 tablespoon grill seasoning blend (Montreal by McCormick)
2 eggs
1 tablespoon milk
2 teaspoons hot sauce
$1/2$ cup all purpose flour
2 to 3 tablespoons oil
4 (6 to 8 ounce) chicken breasts

Preheat oven to 350 degrees. Place nuts, bread crumbs and grill seasoning in food processor and pulse-grind to combine. Pour mixture onto plate and set aside. Beat eggs with milk and hot sauce in shallow dish; set aside. Pour flour on a plate; set aside. Preheat a nonstick skillet over medium-high heat. Add oil to coat the bottom of pan with a thin layer. Dip chicken pieces in egg mixture, coat with flour, then coat again with nut mixture. Brown chicken 2 minutes on each side in hot oil or until light golden in color. Transfer to a baking sheet and finish cooking in oven until juices run clear and breasts are cooked through, about 10 to 12 minutes.

"Delicious. Even my picky young children will eat this."

Vicki Pearl   Townsend Junior High School, Chino Hills, CA

Italian Chicken Pockets

Serves 6

$3/4$ pound boneless skinless chicken breast, cubed
2 tablespoons olive oil
1 (medium) green pepper, chopped
1 cup fresh mushrooms, sliced
1 (3.5 ounce) package sliced pepperoni
1 cup spaghetti sauce
3 (6 ") whole wheat pita breads, halved and warmed
Parmesan cheese, grated

In a large skillet, sauté chicken in oil until no longer pink. Add the green pepper and mushrooms; cook until tender. Stir in pepperoni; heat through. Drain. Stir in spaghetti sauce; heat through. Spoon into pita bread halves. Sprinkle with Parmesan cheese.

"This is a delicious hot sandwich that can be ready in 15 minutes.
I sometimes substitute French rolls for the pita bread."

Cheri Schuette   Valley View Middle School, Simi Valley, CA

Jan's Shrimpy Chicken

Makes 4

4 boneless, skinless chicken breasts
1 egg, beaten
bread crumbs
Filling:
baby tiger shrimp (may be frozen)
cream of chicken soup
1 to 2 tablespoons dill weed
3 green onions, finely chopped

Blend filling ingredients together. Dip chicken breast in beaten egg, fill with 1/4 filling and roll in bread crumbs. Place seam side down in baking dish. Repeat with remaining chicken breasts. Bake at 450 degrees for 20 minutes.

"This is one of those very elegant looking dishes that nobody needs to know was really easy!"

Janis Schulenburg   Irvine High School, Irvine, CA

Malibu Chicken

Serves 6

6 breaded chicken patties, frozen
6 slices ham
6 slices Swiss cheese
1 1/2 cups mayonnaise
2 tablespoons mustard

Preheat oven to 350 degrees. Bake chicken patties as directed on package. When finished baking, place 1 slice ham and 1 slice cheese on each patty. Return to oven until cheese melts. Mix mayonnaise and mustard together for sauce to serve with chicken.

"Usually the frozen chicken patties take approximately 10 minutes to cook. The breaded chicken patties can be used for a lot of different, quick recipes."

Debi Weiss   Ayala High School, Chino Hills, CA

Mexican Turkey Sandwiches
Serves 6

$^2/_3$ cup light cream cheese, softened
$^1/_4$ cup onion, chopped
$^1/_4$ cup salsa + 6 tablespoons, no salt added, divided
2 tablespoons olives, chopped
6 (6") flour tortillas
10 ounces smoked turkey breast, thinly sliced
$^1/_2$ cup fat free cheddar cheese, shredded
1 cup curly leaf lettuce, thinly sliced

Beat cream cheese with a mixer at medium speed until smooth. Add chopped onion, $^1/_4$ cup salsa and olives; stirring well. Spread mixture evenly over tortillas; top evenly with turkey, salsa, cheese and lettuce. Roll up tortillas, jelly roll fashion. Wrap sandwiches individually with plastic wrap. Chill at least 2 hours.

"This makes a great meal or can be served as a side dish."

Toni Purtill   Basic High School, Henderson, NV

Mushroom Chicken
Serves 6 - 8

6 chicken breasts, skinned, boned, halved
1 (10.5 ounce) can cream of mushroom soup
1 cup sour cream
$^1/_8$ teaspoon black pepper
2 tablespoons parsley, chopped
1 cup mushrooms, sliced

Preheat oven to 350 degrees. Arrange chicken breasts in a 9" x 13" baking dish. Mix remaining ingredients together in a bowl. Pour over chicken and bake 1 hour or until chicken is slightly browned and thoroughly cooked.

"Simple and great for company. Serve with a seasoned rice."

Susan Lefler   Ramona Junior High School, Chino, CA

Mustard Coated Chicken Breasts
Serves 4

3 tablespoons Dijon mustard
3 tablespoons olive oil
2 cloves garlic, minced
$^1/_2$ teaspoon dried tarragon
4 boneless, skinless chicken breasts
salt and pepper, to taste
2 cups whole wheat bread crumbs (freshly made are best)

Preheat oven to 450 degrees. Lightly oil heavy baking sheet. Mix together Dijon mustard, olive oil, garlic and tarragon. Season chicken with salt and pepper. Spread mustard mixture on both sides of chicken. Dip chicken into bread crumbs, turning to coat completely. Place chicken on prepared baking sheet. Bake until chicken is cooked through and crumb coating is golden brown, about 14 minutes.

"This is a family favorite at our house. I make my own bread crumbs by toasting bread and putting it through the food processor."

Debbie Grove   Piner High School, Santa Rosa, CA

Oven Fried Chicken
Serves 4

$3/4$ cup lowfat buttermilk
2 chicken breast halves, about 1 pound, skinned
2 chicken drumsticks, skinned
2 chicken thighs, skinned
$1/2$ cup all-purpose flour
1 teaspoon salt
$1/2$ teaspoon ground red pepper
$1/4$ teaspoon white pepper
$1/4$ teaspoon ground cumin
nonstick cooking spray

Combine first 4 ingredients in a large ziploc bag; seal and refrigerate at least 1 hour, turning occasionally. Preheat oven to 450 degrees. Combine flour, salt, peppers and cumin in a second ziploc bag. Remove chicken from first bag, discarding marinade. Add chicken, one piece at a time, to flour mixture, shaking bag to coat chicken. Remove chicken from bag, shaking off excess flour; lightly coat each piece with cooking spray. Return chicken, one piece at a time, to flour mixture, shaking bag to coat each piece. Place on baking sheet that has been lined with parchment paper. Lightly coat chicken with cooking spray. Bake 35 minutes or until done, turning after 20 minutes.

"Marinating in buttermilk results in tender, juicy chicken and double breading gives a crisp crust. For a smoky taste, use ground chipolte pepper in place of ground red pepper. Each serving is only 286 calories and 4.4 grams of fat!"

Jeri Lundy   Grossmont High School, La Mesa, CA

Oven Fried Chicken Sticks with Honey Mustard Sauce
Serves 6

2 $1/2$ pounds boneless, skinless chicken breasts
$3/4$ cup butter, melted
1 teaspoon salt, divided
$1/4$ teaspoon pepper
1 cup corn flakes, coarsely crushed
1 cup mayonnaise
$1/3$ cup Dijon mustard
2 teaspoons honey

Preheat oven to 425 degrees. Grease two shallow baking pans. Gently pound chicken between sheets of plastic wrap until $1/2$" thick. Cut chicken lengthwise into $1/2$" wide strips. Stir together butter, $3/4$ teaspoon salt and pepper in shallow pan. Put corn flakes in another shallow pan. Working with one strip at a time, dip in butter, then dredge in corn flakes. Place on baking pans and bake 15 minutes. Meanwhile, prepare sauce by combining mayonnaise, Dijon mustard, honey and remaining $1/4$ teaspoon salt.

"Honey mustard sauce tastes good with this.
The strips can also be put on wooden skewers for appetizers."

Janice Tuttle   Mills High School, Millbrae, CA

Pepper Jack Chicken
Serves 4 - 6

1 chicken breast, per person
1 $1/2$ teaspoon salt
1 $1/2$ teaspoons cumin
1 $1/2$ teaspoons chili powder
12 ounces jack cheese with jalapeño peppers
$1/2$ cup flour or bread crumbs
1 to 3 tablespoons oil

Place chicken breast between 2 pieces of waxed paper. Using a rolling pin, flatten to $1/4$" thick. Repeat with remaining chicken breasts. In a small bowl, combine salt, cumin and chili powder; mix well. Sprinkle each side of chicken breast with mixture. Place a slice of cheese in center of each chicken breast and roll up, securing with a toothpick. Refrigerate 1 to 24 hours. Sprinkle each breast with flour or bread crumbs. Heat 1 tablespoon oil in a skillet over medium heat. Brown chicken breast, and continue to cook about 20 minutes or until chicken is done, and not pink in the middle. Place in oven to keep warm.

Toni Purtill   Basic High School, Henderson, NV

Pineapple Chicken
Serves 4

1 pound boneless chicken, cut in small cubes or 1" slices
1 tablespoon cornstarch
1 teaspoon salt
1 tablespoon soy sauce
2 teaspoons water
2 tablespoons oil, divided
1 onion, sliced
2 or 3 stalks celery, sliced
1 (8 ounce) can water chestnuts, sliced
1 (20 ounce) can pineapple chunks, drained (reserve juice)
2 cups hot, cooked rice

Marinate chicken in mixture of cornstarch, salt, soy sauce and water. Set aside while you prepare vegetables. Heat 1 tablespoon oil in wok or fry pan and sauté onion, celery and water chestnuts for 2 minutes or less. Keep stirring. Remove from pan. Add 1 tablespoon oil and sauté marinated chicken until browned. Keep stirring. Add vegetables, pineapple chunks and 4 tablespoons reserved pineapple juice to the chicken; simmer until thoroughly heated. Serve immediately with hot rice.

"This is always a hit at school. It is fast and delicious."

Faith Gobuty   Woodside High School, Woodside , CA

Quick Fried Fillets

Serves 4

1 to 2 pounds boneless, skinless chicken or
   turkey fillets or cutlets, thinly sliced
$1/4$ cup milk
$3/4$ cup bread crumbs, plain or seasoned
2 tablespoons oil or nonstick cooking spray
salt, pepper, garlic salt (optional)

Rinse and pat dry the fillets. Place milk in bowl. Place bread crumbs in another bowl. Dip fillets in milk, then in bread crumbs, coating both sides. Heat Teflon pan with oil or spray with nonstick cooking spray over medium heat. Place cutlets in pan and season meat. Cook until lightly browned, about 6 minutes. Turn over and season other side. Cook until browned and tender, approximately 6 minutes. Serve immediately.

Jane Greaves   Central High School West, Fresno, CA

Ritz Cracker Chicken

Serves 6

8 boneless, skinless chicken breasts
nonstick cooking spray
2 cups Ritz crackers, crushed
3 tablespoons Parmesan cheese, grated
2 teaspoons garlic salt or powder
1 teaspoon salt
1 (8 ounce) container plain yogurt
$1/2$ cup butter or margarine, melted

Preheat oven to 350 degrees. Remove any excess fat from chicken and pat dry. Spray a 9" x 13" baking dish with nonstick cooking spray. Combine crackers, cheese, garlic salt or powder and salt in a bowl. In another bowl, coat each chicken breast in yogurt, then coat in cracker mixture. Place coated chicken in baking dish. Drizzle top of chicken with melted butter or margarine and bake, uncovered, 45 minutes.

"Great flavor, tender and moist... a family favorite."

Teresa Watson   Don Juan Avila Middle School, Aliso Viejo, CA

Stir-Fry Chicken & Vegetables
Serves 4

$1/2$ pound chicken, cooked, cut into $1/2$" cubes
3 tablespoons soy sauce
1 teaspoon rice or white vinegar
$1/4$ teaspoon ground cumin
2 cloves garlic, minced
$1/8$ teaspoon ground ginger
3 tablespoons peanut or salad oil
1 (large) carrot, chopped
2 cups broccoli, chopped
1 cup bean sprouts
1 cup mushrooms, sliced
$1/2$ cup green onions, sliced
3 tablespoons cilantro, minced

Place cubed chicken in a bowl. In a small bowl, mix soy sauce with vinegar, cumin, garlic and ginger; drizzle over chicken and set aside to marinate. Heat oil in wok or frying pan over high heat. Sauté chicken. Add carrot and stir fry 1 minute. Add broccoli and stir fry 2 minutes more. Mix in bean sprouts, mushrooms and green onions. Stir fry 30 more seconds, reduce heat and cook 1 to 2 minutes more. Garnish with cilantro.

"Serve this with white steamed rice and you have a very healthy meal!
Also, have fun experimenting with different vegetables and the chicken
can be substituted with tofu for a vegetarian alternative."

Melissa Webb   Lakewood High School, Lakewood, CA

Sweet & Sour Chicken
Serves 4

3 tablespoons corn starch
1 $1/2$ cups brown sugar (packed)
$2/3$ cup vinegar
2 tablespoons soy sauce
1 cup pineapple, crushed or tidbits
$1/2$ cup green peppers, chopped
12 to 15 chicken tender strips

Preheat oven to 375 degrees. Mix corn starch and brown sugar together in sauce pan. Stir in the vinegar, soy sauce, pineapple and green peppers. Boil 3 to 5 minutes. Wash chicken and place in a 9" x 13" casserole dish that has been sprayed with nonstick cooking spray. Pour sauce over chicken and bake 40 minutes, stirring occasionally while cooking.

"This is a really good sweet and sour recipe.
It can also be used with meatballs or pork."

Camille Hicks   Riverton High School, Riverton, UT

Sweet & Sour Chicken with Rice

Serves 4

1 (16 ounce) can Contadina Sweet & Sour Sauce
8 ounces water
4 (4 ounce) boneless, skinless chicken breasts
2 tablespoons margarine
6 ounces Rice-A-Roni Fried Rice
2 cups water

Pour Contadina Sweet & sour sauce into a large pan. Add 8 ounces water to sauce and stir. Heat to a simmer and add the chicken breasts; simmer 45 minutes. Meanwhile, melt margarine in a small saucepan. Add Rice-A-Roni and brown. Add 2 cups water, stir, cover and simmer 15 minutes. Serve cooked chicken over hot rice.

"Quick, convenient and allows time to assist children with homework!"

Jill Sweet-Gregory   Santa Paula High School, Santa Paula, CA

Tangy Citrus Chicken

Serves 8

8 boneless, skinless chicken breast halves (about 2-$1/2$ pounds)
1 (6 ounce) can frozen lemonade concentrate, thawed
$1/2$ cup honey
1 teaspoon rubbed sage
$1/2$ teaspoon ground mustard
$1/2$ teaspoon dried thyme
$1/2$ teaspoon lemon juice

Preheat oven to 350 degrees. Place chicken breasts in a 9" x 13" x 2" baking dish coated with nonstick cooking spray. In a small bowl, combine remaining ingredients; mix well. Pour half over the chicken. Bake, uncovered, 20 minutes. Turn chicken; pour remaining sauce on top. Bake 15 to 20 minutes longer, or until meat juices run clear.

"I came across this recipe from the National Honey Board a few years ago. It is amazingly quick and easy."

Cindy Peters   Deer Valley High School, Antioch, CA

Turkey and Black Bean Wraps

Makes 8   **(Photo opposite page 65)**

2 (medium) tomatoes, chopped
$1/_2$ cup black beans, rinsed, drained
4 tablespoons diced green chiles
$1/_3$ cup green onions, sliced
1 tablespoon fresh cilantro, chopped
water
1 (1.27 ounce) package Lawry's Fajitas Spices & Seasonings
3 cups turkey, cooked, shredded or diced
8 (large) Mission flour tortillas, warmed to soften

In medium bowl, combine tomatoes, black beans, chiles, green onion and cilantro; set aside. In large skillet, stir together water and Fajitas Spices & Seasonings; bring to a boil. Stir in turkey and reduce heat to low. Mix in tomato mixture and cook on low for 5 minutes or until turkey is thoroughly cooked, stirring occasionally. Scoop $1/_2$ cup filling on each tortilla. Fold in sides and roll up to enclose filling. Note: May substitute cooked chicken or pork for turkey.

Lawry's Foods, Inc.   **www.lawrys.com**

Apple Pecan Tenderloin Medallions

Serves 4

> 1 pound pork tenderloin
> 2 tablespoons butter
> 1 (16 ounce) can sliced apples, drained
> $^1/_4$ cup brown sugar, packed
> $^1/_2$ cup pecans, chopped

Trim fat from pork. Cut into $^1/_2$" thick slices. Melt butter in a large skillet over medium-high heat until it sizzles. Reduce heat to medium. Arrange pork slices in skillet. Cook 2 minutes; turn slices. Spoon apples over pork. Sprinkle with brown sugar and pecans. Cover and cook 4 to 6 minutes more.

National Pork Board   www.theotherwhitemeat.com

Mediterranean Pasta Salad

Serves 4

$3/4$ pound peppered pork roast, cooked, cut into thin strips

12 ounces penne or ziti pasta, cooked, drained

1 (small) cucumber, diced

6 ounces feta cheese, crumbled

1 cup cherry tomatoes, halved

$1/2$ cup fresh mint leaves, chopped

$1/2$ cup Greek vinaigrette dressing

In large bowl, gently toss all ingredients with dressing. Serve on shallow salad bowls or dinner plates.

National Pork Board   **www.theotherwhitemeat.com**

Main Dishes *with* Pork

24-Hour Breakfast
Serves 12

12 slices bread, cubed
$1/2$ pound (2 cups) cheese, grated, divided
2 to 3 cups ham or sausage, cooked, cubed
8 eggs
2 cups milk
1 teaspoon salt
$1/2$ cup butter, melted

Grease a 9" x 13" baking dish. Place half the bread cubes on bottom. Cover with half of the cheese and ham or sausage. Repeat layers. In a medium mixing bowl, combine eggs, milk and salt. Pour over casserole and drizzle with melted butter; refrigerate overnight. Bake at 350 degrees, uncovered for 1 hour, 15 minutes.

"Great for overnight guests!"

Joy Sweeney-Aiello   Porterville High School, Porterville, CA

Apple Pecan Tenderloin Medallions
Serves 4   (Photo opposite page 96)

1 pound pork tenderloin
2 tablespoons butter
1 (16 ounce) can sliced apples, drained
$1/4$ cup brown sugar, packed
$1/2$ cup pecans, chopped

Trim fat from pork. Cut into $1/2$" thick slices. Melt butter in a large skillet over medium-high heat until it sizzles. Reduce heat to medium. Arrange pork slices in skillet. Cook 2 minutes; turn slices. Spoon apples over pork. Sprinkle with brown sugar and pecans. Cover and cook 4 to 6 minutes more.

National Pork Board   www.theotherwhitemeat.com

Bacon Avocado Quesadillas
Serves 2-4

8 bacon strips, diced
$1/2$ pound fresh mushrooms, sliced
1 tablespoon margarine, softened
4 (7 ") flour tortillas
2 cups Monterey jack cheese, shredded
1 (medium) tomato, chopped
1 ripe avocado, peeled and sliced
Sour cream and salsa

In a large skillet, cook the bacon until crisp. Remove to paper towels and drain. Sauté mushrooms in 1 teaspoon of reserved bacon drippings. Spread butter over one side of each tortilla. Place two tortillas, buttered side down on a griddle. Top with bacon, mushrooms, cheese, tomato and avocado. Cover with remaining tortillas, buttered side up. Cook over low heat for 1 to 2 minutes or until golden brown. Turn and cook 1 to 2 minutes longer or until the cheese is melted. Cut into wedges. Serve with sour cream and salsa.

Cheri Schuette   Valley View Middle School, Simi Valley, CA

BBQ Style Pork Sandwiches
Serves 6

2 (large) green peppers, cut into strips
1 (large) onion, thinly sliced, separated into rings
2 tablespoons quick cooking tapioca
1 (2 to 3 pound) pork shoulder roast
1 (10.5 ounce) can condensed tomato soup
2 tablespoons steak sauce
3 to 4 teaspoons chili powder
$1/2$ teaspoon sugar
$1/4$ teasoon garlic powder
$1/4$ teasoon pepper
1 tablespoon Tabasco sauce
6 to 8 kaiser rolls, split

Crockpot RECIPE!

In a 3 quart or larger crockpot combine green pepper and onions. Sprinkle tapioca over vegetables. Trim fat from roast. Place roast atop vegetables. In a medium bowl, combine tomato soup, steak sauce, chili powder, sugar, garlic powder, pepper and Tabasco. Pour over roast in crockpot. Cover and cook on low heat setting 10 to 12 hours or on high setting 5 to 6 hours. Remove roast from cooker and thinly slice or shred meat. Skim fat from sauce. Serve meat on kaiser rolls; top with BBQ sauce and serve.

"This recipe is great for game days. A real crowd pleaser.
A side of coleslaw either homemade or from the deli completes this meal."

Patti Bartholomew   Casa Roble High School, Orangevale, CA

BBQ'd Pork & Coke Sandwiches

Serves 6-8

Crockpot
RECIPE!

3 pound pork loin
1 (12 ounce) jar of your favorite barbecue sauce
1 can Coke, not diet
1 package Hawaiian sandwich rolls

Place pork loin in a crockpot and cover with barbecue sauce. Cook on low 6 to 8 hours. Shred pork and return to sauce. Add can of Coke. Cook one more hour on high, uncovered. Serve on Hawaiian rolls.

"Make sure you use your favorite barbecue sauce to get the best flavor. My family loves this for dinner and leftovers the next day."

Mary Nafis   Montclair High School, Montclair, CA

Breakfast Hash Browns & Eggs

Serves 8

1 (large) bag frozen hash browns
salt and pepper, to taste
1 cube butter or margarine
1 cup sausage or bacon, cooked, crumbled
8 eggs
$1/4$ cup milk
1 cup cheese, shredded

Preheat oven to 350 degrees. Place hash browns in a 9" x 13" dish. Salt and pepper. Drizzle with melted butter or margarine. Bake until tender, about 20 minutes. Remove from oven and top with crumbled bacon or sausage. Whisk eggs with milk and pour over top. Sprinkle cheese on top and return to oven for 20 minutes longer.

"Great for Christmas morning!"

Karyn Hobbs   Lemoore High School, Lemoore, CA

Chile Verde

Serves 4 - 6

2 tablespoons oil, divided
2 pounds pork tenderloin, cut into $1/2$" cubes
1 (20 ounce) can green chile enchilada sauce
1 (4 ounce) can green chiles, chopped
$1/2$ teaspoon salt
$1/4$ teaspoon pepper
tortillas
grated cheese

Preheat large frying pan over medium heat; add 1 tablespoon oil and half of pork cubes. Brown meat on all sides. Remove meat from pan and add remaining oil; repeat with remaining pork cubes. Return all meat to frying pan; add enchilada sauce, chiles, salt and pepper. Stir well and bring to a boil;

reduce heat and simmer about 20 minutes, until sauce thickens and meat is cooked through. Serve warm with tortillas and grated cheese.

"This is an easy entrée. Serve with a green salad."

Beth Guerrero   Selma High School, Selma, CA

Fireman's Breakfast Casserole
Serves 2 - 3

> 6 to 8 hash brown squares, frozen (with or without cheese)
> 1 pound bacon, sausage or ham, cooked, crumbled,
>   (or a combination of any)
> 6 eggs, beaten
> 1 cup cheese, shredded
> onions, chiles, salsa, peppers, as desired

Preheat oven to 350 degrees. Line a 9" x 13" pan with frozen hash brown squares. Spread the cooked crumbled meat on top. Pour beaten eggs over and top with cheese and anything else desired. Bake 35 minutes.

"Our friend and fire chief of Newport Fire Station, Randy Schurer, would make this when our families would camp together. Firemen know how to cook!"

Debbie Farr   Foothill High School, Santa Ana, CA

Green Chile Pork
Serves 8-10

> 4 pound pork loin roast
> 2 cans diced green chiles
> 1 large can Hatch green enchilada sauce
> 1 cup Herdez salsa
> 2 cloves garlic
> 1 onion, chopped
> salt and pepper to taste

Crockpot RECIPE!

Slice onion and place in crockpot. Put pork roast on top of onions. Pour all remaining ingredients over roast. Cover and cook on low 7 to 8 hours. Shred meat and serve on tortillas.

"This crockpot dish is so easy and so delicious. I often put the ingredients in the crock the night before and store it in the fridge. Then before I leave for work, I simply put the crock in the heating element, plug it in and head out the door. When I get home, dinner is served!"

Kristine Haas   West Jordan High School, West Jordan, Utah

Ham & Swiss Stromboli

Serves 6

1 (11 ounce) tube refrigerated French bread
6 ounces deli ham, thinly sliced
6 green onions, sliced
8 strips bacon, cooked, crumbled
1 $1/2$ cups (6 ounces) Swiss cheese, shredded

Preheat oven to 350 degrees. Unroll dough on a greased baking sheet. Place ham over dough to within $1/2$" of edges; sprinkle evenly with onions, bacon and cheese. Roll up jelly-roll style, starting with long side. Pinch seams to seal and tuck ends under. Place seam side down on baking sheet. With a sharp knife, cut several $1/4$" deep slits on top of loaf. Bake 26 to 30 minutes or until golden brown. Cool slightly before slicing. Serve warm.

"This tastes like a delicious Quizno's sub–warm and toasty!"

Carole Delap   Golden West High School, Visalia, CA

Italian Sausage & Vegetables

Serves 3

8 sweet or hot Italian sausage links
1 (large) green pepper, quartered
2 (large) tomatoes, quartered
$1/2$ pound mushrooms, halved or left whole
1 (large) onion, quartered
garlic salt
basil leaves
parsley flakes
pepper and salt, to taste
1 pound spinach noodles

Boil sausage in water for 10 minutes, cool and cut into 1" pieces and brown in skillet. Cover and cook 20 minutes. Place vegetables in a large bowl and toss with seasonings, to taste. Cook spinach noodles according to package directions; drain. Place vegetables in with sausage and turn up heat for 7 to 8 minutes. Serve vegetables over hot buttered noodles.

"This is very colorful and delicious."

Janis Schulenburg   Irvine High School, Irvine, CA

Kris's Fettuccini

Serves 4 - 6

1 to 1 $1/2$ pounds fettuccini (6 cups cooked)
2 sweet or mild Italian sausages
2 hot Italian sausages
2 cloves garlic, minced
2 teaspoons olive oil
$1/2$ cup red bell pepper, thinly sliced
$1/2$ cup dry white wine or chicken broth
$1/4$ teaspoon crushed red chiles (optional)
$1/4$ cup tomato sauce
4 cups whipping cream or 4 cups milk
2 tablespoons all-purpose flour
salt and pepper, to taste
$1/4$ cup Italian parsley, minced
Parmesan cheese, thinly shaved

Place 3 to 4 quarts water in 5 to 6 quart pan over high heat; cover with lid and bring water to a boil. Meanwhile, pierce sausages in several places with fork. In 10" to 12" skillet, over medium-high heat, lightly brown sausages, 5 to 8 minutes. Set sausages on a plate and cut into $1/2$" thick rounds. Wipe frying pan clean, return to heat and add garlic and olives oil; stir until lightly browned, about 2 minutes. Return sausages and any juices to pan along with bell peppers, wine or broth, chiles and tomato sauce. On high heat, stir several times until liquid comes to full roiling boil. Let boil about 2 minutes. Stir flour into cream or milk and add to boiling mixture, stirring until sauce returns to a full rolling boil. Stir and boil about 1 minute. Season to taste with salt and pepper to taste. To boiling water, add pasta and stir several times to prevent sticking. Cook, uncovered, until pasta is tender to bite. Drain at once then pour into large bowl. Pour sauce onto pasta and toss until sauce is absorbed (mixture should be slightly soupy). Serve pasta and sauce in shallow bowls, sprinkled with parsley and Parmesan. Add salt and pepper, if desired, to taste.

"Serve with a salad and French bread. A winter favorite - goes together easily."
Kris Hawkins   Clovis West High School, Fresno, CA

McAuley Surprise
Serves 4 - 5

1 pound ground beef
1 (12 ounce) package Jimmy Dean original sausage
2 to 3 cloves garlic, minced
1 (small) onion, diced
1 can Italian stewed tomatoes with juice
1 package frozen spinach, thawed, squeezed dry, coarsely chopped
2 teaspoons Italian seasoning
4 eggs, beaten
Parmesan cheese, grated

Sauté and brown beef with sausage, garlic and onion. Add stewed tomatoes with juice, and spinach. Cook about 10 minutes and most liquid will evaporate. Add seasoning. Make a well in cnter of mixture and pour in eggs. Scramble slightly, mixing with ingredients. Serve hot, topped with a sprinkling of Parmesan cheese.

"Great one-pan meal–add a salad and a loaf of French bread!"
Gail McAuley   Lincoln High School, Stockton, CA

Microwave Egg McMuffin
Serves 1

1 (large) egg
1 English muffin, split
1 slice American cheese
1 slice ham or Canadian bacon
nonstick cooking spray

Spray small microwave safe dish with cooking spray. Crack egg into dish and pierce yolk with fork. Cover dish with paper towel. Microwave on high 30 seconds. Pierce yolk again using fork. Microwave additional 20 to 30 seconds. Assemble: Place egg, slice of cheese and slice of ham on one half of muffin. Wrap in paper towel and microwave on high 25 seconds. Let stand 1 minute before eating.

"This is a delicious and speedy breakfast. This is a favorite of my students, which I often use when teaching units on microwave use, the importance of nutritious breakfast and eggs! It's great served with Orange Julius."
Leigh Ann Diffenderfer   Newbury Park High School, Newbury Park, CA

Muffy's Baked Eggs in a Ring

Serves 1

1 slice bacon
1 egg
$1/2$ teaspoon butter
salt and pepper, to taste
1 English muffin, split, toasted
1 slice cheese

Partially cook bacon; place inside muffin tin around the edge. Crack egg and pour into muffin tin, inside bacon ring. Top with butter, salt and pepper. Bake at 350 degrees for 17 to 20 minutes. Remove from oven and place on half of English muffin. Top with slice of cheese and remaining half of muffin. Wait 3 to 4 minutes while cheese melts.

"Who needs the Golden Arches when you can make it yourself!"

Julie Ericksen   Skyline High School, Salt Lake City, UT

Pizza Joes

Serves 4

4 French sandwich rolls, split
4 ounces pizza sauce
2 ounces pepperoni, sliced
4 slices Mozzarella cheese
2 to 3 tablespoons Parmesan cheese, grated

Preheat oven to 350 degrees. Spread each side of sandwich rolls with pizza sauce. On bottom half of roll, place 3 to 4 slices pepperoni, cover with 1 slice mozzarella cheese. Sprinkle with Parmesan cheese. Top with upper half of roll. Wrap in foil and heat 20 to 25 minutes. Filling should be hot and cheese melted.

Alice Claiborne   Fairfield High School, Fairfield, CA

Quick Creamy Parmesan Pasta

Serves 4 - 6

1 (small) package angel hair pasta
1 package button mushrooms, sliced
2 tablespoons butter
salt, to taste
white pepper, to taste
5 thin slices panchetta, diced
$1/2$ pint heavy cream
5 tablespoons quality Parmesan cheese, grated, divided

Cook pasta according to the package directions, just to al dente. Drain and keep in the colander. Meanwhile, sauté mushrooms in butter over medium heat, being sure not to scorch the butter. Season with salt and pepper to taste while cooking. Drain any liquid which accumulates in the bottom of pan.

Pour cream over the mushrooms, add the panchetta and simmer until the cream begins to thicken, about 5 to 6 minutes. Add the pasta to the skillet. Toss until coated with sauce and heated through. Check the seasoning, adding more salt and pepper if needed. Toss with 3 tablespoons Parmesan. Serve, topped with a remaining 2 tablespoons Parmesan.

"This recipe was given to me by a student a few years ago. While this is not exactly low fat, it is delicious and quick. Serve with a spinach salad and it's really excellent."
Delaine Smith   West Valley High School, Cottonwood, CA

Rice & Ham Medley
Serves 4

    3 cups (any flavor) Rice-A-Roni, cooked
    2 cups cooked ham, chopped
    1 (medium) green pepper, chopped
    1 (medium) red pepper, chopped
    1 (medium) onion, chopped

Cook rice according to package directions; set aside. In large skillet, sauté onion and peppers until tender. Add ham and cooked rice and stir until heated through.

"Add a green salad and dinner is ready in 45 minutes!"
Karen Tilson   Poly High School, Riverside, CA

Slow Cooker BBQ Pork
Serves 6

    3 to 5 pound pork loin
    3/4 cup Trader Joe's Kansas City BBQ sauce
      (or your favorite BBQ sauce)
    1 to 2 yellow onions, quartered
    1 jalapeño or serrano chile pepper, seeded and sliced
    3 garlic cloves, sliced

Crockpot
RECIPE!

Put all ingredients in a crockpot and cook on low heat 6 to 8 hours. You can put the chile and garlic in whole if you don't have time. After it's cooked, shred the meat and stir to combine all ingredients.

"This tastes great and it's low fat. My husband and I love this on days we don't want to cook. I serve it with baked beans, flour tortillas, and salsa. It's also great on a bed of rice topped with diced tomatoes and green onions. It can be put together the night before in a removable crockpot dish and saved in the refrigerator."
Holly Pittman   El Capitan High School, Lakeside, CA

Main Dishes with Seafood

Cheesy Tuna Noodles

Serves 4-5

$1/4$ cup onion, chopped
$1/4$ cup green pepper, chopped
1 tablespoon butter
1 can cheddar cheese soup (condensed)
$1/2$ cup milk
3 $1/2$ to 4 cups wide egg noodles, cooked, drained
1 can tuna in water, drained

Sauté onion and green pepper in butter. Stir in soup and milk, stirring to combine. Add noodles and tuna and heat through. Serve immediately.

"I am a busy mom of 3, when I have had a very busy day I know that this recipe is a winner because it is very quick and easy to prepare. I keep chopped green pepper and chopped onion in the freezer so it is on always hand. Other ways to combat dinner time rush hour is to precook hamburger and chicken for those recipes that call for cooked hamburger and chicken. I buy hamburger in large amounts and cook it on a cookie sheet, cover with foil and cook in the oven at 350 degrees for about 20 min. Be sure that you test to make sure it is no longer pink inside. For easy cleanup I line the cookie sheet with foil. I then drain and rinse the hamburger and put it back on the cookie sheet, put it in the freezer for 20 minutes, then take it out and put it in a freezer bag. This way when you can use some of it with out it being all stuck together. I do the same thing with chicken. I bake it or cook in boiling water with some buillon, cut or chop and freeze as with the hamburger. This may take some planning and a little extra time after shopping but it saves much time. When making casseroles I make 2 and put one in the freezer for later."

Gaylene Greenwood

Roy High School, Roy, UT

Fish Tacos

Serves 4 servings

3/4 pound tilapia, red snapper, or other fresh fish fillets
1/2 cup salsa
8 corn tortillas
2 cups lettuce or cabbage, shredded
1 tomato, chopped
1 cup cheddar and/or jack cheese, shredded
Optional: 1/2 avocado, chopped; additional salsa

In a heavy skillet lightly sprayed with vegetable cooking spray, over medium heat, place fish fillets one layer deep. Cook 2 minutes and turn fish to other side. Cook 2 minutes more. Pour 1/2 cup salsa over top of fish. Cover skillet with a lid and turn heat to lowest temperature for about 4 minutes. Remove lid and allow liquid to evaporate. Heat tortillas on a griddle or wrapped in a towel in the microwave for 30 seconds. Fill each tortilla with 1/8 of the fish, lettuce, tomato, and cheese. Serve with avocado and additional salsa if desired.

"To speed the preparation, buy coleslaw mix and packaged shredded cheese. My family enjoys refried beans in the tacos too."

Linda Falkenstien   Morro Bay High School, Morro Bay, CA

Ginger & Garlic Glazed Salmon

Serves 2

nonstick cooking spray
2 (6 ounce) salmon fillets, 1" thick
3 tablespoons bottled ginger & garlic marinade

Preheat broiler. Place salmon, skin side down, on a broiler pan that has been coated with nonstick cooking spray. Brush with marinade. Broil 10 to 12 minutes or until fish flakes easily when tested with fork.

"Experiment with different types of marinade."

Joye Cantrell   Rialto High School, Rialto, CA

Grilled or Broiled Fish Steaks

Serves 3 - 4

1 to 1 1/2 pounds fish fillets (salmon, halibut, shark)
1/2 cup olive oil
1/4 cup soy sauce
1/2 teaspoon dried dill weed
2 tablespoons lemon juice
dash of ground clove

Mix all ingredients and brush on fish. Broil or grill about 3 to 4 minutes on each side.

"This is so fast. I serve it with rice and a good salad."

Pat Hufnagel   Esperanza High School, Anaheim, CA

Grilled Sea Bass

Serves 6

$1/4$ teaspoon garlic powder
$1/4$ teaspoon onion powder
$1/4$ teaspoon paprika
lemon pepper, to taste
sea salt, to taste
2 pounds sea bass
3 tablespoons butter
2 (large) cloves garlic, chopped
1 tablespoon Italian flat leaf parsley, chopped
1 $1/2$ tablespoons extra virgin olive oil

Lightly oil grill grate, then preheat grill for high heat. In a small bowl, stir together garlic powder, onion powder, paprika, lemon pepper and sea salt. Sprinkle seasonings over fish. In a small saucepan over medium heat, melt butter with garlic and parsley. Remove from heat when butter has melted and set aside. Grill fish for 7 minutes, then turn and drizzle with butter. Continue cooking for 7 minutes, or until easily flaked with a fork. Drizzle with olive oil before serving.

"This is a truly flavorful dish with a lovely plate presentation. My mom and I experimented and made this for lunch. It came out so good I promptly went to the fish market so I could make it for my dinner guests that night. Yummy! Prep and cook time, approximately 20 minutes each. Ready to eat in 40 minutes!"

Stephanie San Sebastian   Central High School, Fresno, CA

Linguine with Shrimp & Feta

Serves 6

16 ounces linguine
1 (16 ounce) bag frozen cooked, peeled shrimp
1 (26-ounce) jar marinara sauce
2 tablespoons Pernod liqueur (or anisette)
$1/3$ pound feta cheese, crumbled
$1/4$ cup fresh basil, chopped

Cook linguine according to package directions. While this is cooking, heat the marinara sauce over medium-low heat. Add the shrimp, Pernod and feta. Cook 5 minutes or until heated through. Toss with the cooked and drained linguine and top with the fresh basil.

"This is a wonderful dish you can pull together in a pinch and it appears to be more difficult than it is. Add your own touch such as crushed red peppers, garlic, etc."

Margo Olsen   Amador Valley High School, Pleasanton, CA

Salsa Fillets

Serves 4

1 pound fresh or frozen fish fillets (orange roughy works well)
1/2 cup water
12 to 16 ounces salsa (purchased-mild, hot etc.)
1/2 teaspoon sugar
1/2 teaspoon instant chicken bouillon granules
1/8 teaspoon pepper (white is best)
Few dashes bottled hot pepper sauce
1 to 2 tablespoons tomato paste

Thaw fish. In an 8" x 8" x 2" baking dish stir in water, salsa, sugar, bouillon granules, pepper and hot pepper sauce. Arrange fish fillets on top with thicker portions toward edges of dish. Turn under any thin portions of fillets to obtain an even thickness of about 1/2". Sprinkle fillets with salt and pepper to taste. Cover with a lid or vented clear plastic wrap. Microwave on high for 6 to 9 minutes or until fish flakes easily with a fork. Carefully transfer fish to a serving platter. Keep warm and covered. For sauce, stir tomato paste into tomato mixture in baking dish. Cook, uncovered, on high about 1 minute or till heated through. Serve sauce over cooked fish fillets.

"High protein and low fat with lots of vitamins.
This is a fish entree I can always get kids to eat."

Renee Wilgus   Red Bluff Union High School, Red Bluff, CA

Scallop Scampi

Serves 8

4 tablespoons margarine
3 cloves garlic, minced
1 (large) onion, minced
1/2 cup dry white wine
1 teaspoon salt
1/4 teaspoon ground black pepper
1/2 cup Romano cheese, grated, divided
1 (10.75 ounce) can chicken broth
1 pound fresh bay scallops
1 pound linguine pasta
1/4 cup fresh parsley, chopped

In a large skillet, melt margarine over medium heat and sauté garlic and onion until translucent. Add wine, salt, pepper and 1/4 cup cheese. Stir in chicken broth and scallops. Increase heat to a boil and gently boil 7 to 8 minutes. Meanwhile, bring a large pot of lightly salted water to a boil. Add pasta and cook 8 to 10 minutes or until al dente; drain. Reduce heat under sauce and add parsley. Place sauce over cooked pasta or stir pasta into sauce. Sprinkle with remaining 1/4 cup cheese. Serve hot.

"This recipe is easy! Serve with a green salad and garlic bread."

Cari Sheridan   Grace Yokley Middle School, Ontario, CA

109

Shae's Favorite Pasta Salad

Serves 4 - 6

1 cup broccoli, frozen
1 cup corn, frozen
1 cup green beans, frozen
1 package tricolor pasta, cooked according to package directions
2 cups shrimp, cooked, peeled, tails removed
1 (small) can black olives, sliced
fresh basil, chopped
salt and pepper, to taste
$1/2$ cup pepper jack cheese, grated
$1/2$ cup cheddar cheese, grated
dressing of your choice

Steam frozen vegetables until tender. Drain cooked pasta and vegetables using a colander. Run cold water over all as they drain to cool. Place into large serving bowl. Add shrimp and olives. Season with fresh basil, salt and pepper; mix thoroughly. Sprinkle with grated cheese and dressing of your choice.

"Serve this with sourdough bread. Sliced salami can be substituted for the shrimp, This makes a great one-dish meal and can be served as leftovers for lunch or dinner the next day."

Marleigh Williams   Corning High School, Corning, CA

Tuna Patty Melt

Serves 4

1 (6.5 to 7 ounce) can tuna, drained, flaked
$1/2$ cup oats (quick or old-fashioned)
$1/3$ cup carrots, shredded
1 egg, beaten
$1/4$ cup mayonnaise
2 tablespoons green onion, sliced
$1/8$ teaspoon salt
dash pepper
1 to 2 tablespoons vegetable oil
1 slice American cheese, cut into 4 triangles

Combine all ingredients except oil and cheese; mix well. Shape to form 4 patties about 3 $1/2$" in diameter. Brown in oil in 12" skillet over medium-high heat for 3 to 4 minutes, or until golden brown; turn and continue cooking another 3 to 4 minutes, placing cheese triangle on each patty during last 2 minutes of cooking. Serve on burger buns with lettuce and tomato, if desired.

Jackie Williams   Prospect High School, Saratoga, CA

Main Dishes without Meat

Best Ever Macaroni & Cheese

Serves 4

8 ounces elbow macaroni
3 tablespoons butter
3 tablespoons enriched flour
2 cups milk
$1/2$ teaspoon salt
dash pepper
2 cups Velveeta cheese, shredded, divided

Preheat oven to 350 degrees. Cook macaroni in boiling salted water until tender; drain. Melt butter, blend in flour. Add milk. Cook and stir until thickened. Add salt and pepper. Add 1 $1/2$ cups cheese, stirring until melted. Place cooked macaroni in an 8" or 9" greased pan. Pour sauce over macaroni. Top with remaining cheese and bake 30 minutes, until hot and bubbly.

"Children and teenagers love this! If you are expecting company with children, it is a sure thing–even as a side dish."

Janet Tingley   Atascadero High School, Atascadero, CA

Black Beans Over Polenta

Serves 4

2 tablespoons vegetable oil
1 onion, chopped
1 clove garlic, minced
1/2 red bell pepper, chopped
1/2 pound ground beef (optional)
1 (14 ounce) can black beans
1/4 cup canned corn
1/4 cup sliced olives
1 cup diced canned tomatoes
2 to 3 teaspoons chili powder, or to taste
1 teaspoon cumin powder
salt, to taste
3 1/4 cups water or chicken broth
1 cup polenta
4 tablespoons butter
1 teaspoon salt
1/2 cup Parmesan or 1 cup cheddar cheese, grated

In skillet, heat oil. Sauté onion, garlic, bell pepper and ground beef, if using, about 5 minutes. Add black beans, corn, olives, tomatoes, chili powder and cumin. Simmer about 20 minutes, stirring occasionally. Adjust salt to taste. Meanwhile, bring water or chicken broth, butter and salt to a boil. Gradually add polenta, stirring constantly to avoid lumping. Cook polenta until water is absorbed, stirring frequently, about 25 minutes. Add cheese and combine thoroughly. Polenta can also be baked by placing ingredients in a 9"x 13" pan; stir until blended and bake at 350 degrees, uncovered, for 50 minutes. Run a fork through the top and cover with cheese; bake 5 to 10 minutes longer.

Susan Schmiedt   Bear Creek High School, Stockton, CA

Calzones

Serves 4 - 5

1 loaf frozen bread dough
prepared spaghetti or pizza sauce
8 ounces mozzarella cheese, shredded
Desired fillings: Chopped onion, pineapple,
    pepperoni, bell pepper, olives, etc.
olive oil
garlic powder

Preheat oven to 450 degrees. Cut defrosted bread dough into 4 or 5 pieces. Flatten each piece of dough to about 6 inches in diameter. Lightly brush each piece with prepared sauce. Put grated cheese and other desired filings onto half of each piece of dough. (Pile it high as cheese will melt.) Fold in half and seal edges by pressing with fork. Place onto a greased baking sheet, then brush tops with olive oil and sprinkle with a little garlic powder on top. Bake 12 to 15 minutes. Serve with additional sauce.

Carol Steele   Arroyo Seco Junior High School, Valencia, CA

Chile Relleno Casserole

Serves 8 -12

1 (1 pound 11 ounce) can sliced green chiles
4 eggs
1 (12 ounce) can evaporated milk
$1/_2$ teaspoon salt
2 tablespoons flour
1 pound cheese, grated (your choice)

Preheat oven to 350 degrees. Spray a glass oblong casserole dish with nonstick cooking spray. Layer green chilies on bottom of dish. In a blender, blend eggs with milk, salt and flour. Pour over layered chiles. Sprinkle grated cheese on top of liquid mixture. Bake 1 hour.

"Quick, easy and delicious! Hardly any clean up!"

Teresa Stahl   Needles High School, Needles, CA

Chili Bake

Serves 6

$1/_3$ cup butter
5 (large) eggs
$1/_2$ cup yellow cornmeal
$3/_4$ cup flour
1 $1/_4$ cups milk
2 (15 ounce) cans chili with beans (no meat)

Preheat oven to 425 degrees. Place butter in a 10" cast iron skillet, put in oven and melt. Combine eggs, cornmeal, flour and milk; mix until smooth. Pour batter into skillet, spoon chili into center of batter, leaving a 1 $1/_2$" margin around the edge. Bake 18 to 20 minutes. Serve immediately.

"Quick and easy–you can add beef or chicken.
Bell peppers, onions and cheese add a nice twist!"

Wendy Duncan   West Covina High School, West Covina, CA

Chili Mac

Serves 4-5

1 box macaroni & cheese mix
$1/4$ cup margarine
$1/4$ cup milk
1 can chili, no meat

Prepare macaroni and cheese according to package directions. Stir in chili and heat through. Serve hot.

"This was a desperation dinner while I was attending night classes. It's fast, easy and really good! Add a quick salad, a piece of fruit and a glass of milk for a balanced dinner."

Pamela Bonilla   Valley View High School, Moreno Valley, CA

Easy Enchiladas

Serves 4

8 corn tortillas
2 cups enchilada sauce (red or green, spicy or mild)
Filling:
4 cups cheese (cheddar or jack), shredded or 2 cups chicken,
    shredded and 2 cups cheese, shredded
$1/2$ cup green onions, sliced
2 to 4 tablespoons green mild chiles, chopped
4 cups iceberg lettuce, shredded

Place $1/2$ cup of cheese aside. Place $1/2$ cup enchilada sauce in the bottom of a glass 7" x 11" baking dish. Heat remaining sauce in shallow skillet. Heat 4 tortillas in the microwave on high for 1 minute. Dip each one in sauce, place on plate and place filling ingredients down the center of each tortilla, dividing evenly. Roll seam side down and place in baking dish. Repeat with remaining tortillas. Pour remaining sauce over enchiladas; Heat in microwave on high for 8 minutes or until thoroughly heated. Serve over shredded lettuce.

"Be creative with sauces and fillings. A great way to use leftovers and it's easy to keep enchilada sauce on hand in the can. This is one of my students' favorites. Imitation crab, jack cheese and green sauce is a great combo too!"

Karen Kendall   Slater Middle School, Santa Rosa, CA

Gourmet Vegetable Frittata

Serves any number desired

2 to 3 eggs per person
1 to 2 tablespoons milk or water per egg
salt and pepper, to taste
1 to 2 tablespoons margarine
Optional: shrimp, thawed
sliced zucchini
chopped onion
fresh garlic, minced
tomato wedges
Parmesan cheese, freshly grated
crushed red pepper

Scramble eggs. Add liquid to eggs (water makes eggs fluffy because of the steam; milk has more fat so eggs will have a richer flavor but less fluff). Add salt and pepper to taste and set aside. Melt margarine in large sauté pan. Heat until it starts to bubble. Keep heat medium to medium-low. Now is the time to sauté any item you want cooked before you add the egg mixture, example: shrimp, zucchini, onion, fresh garlic, tomato. Add items that are more dense first and softer item, like tomatoes, last. If using frozen shrimp, defrost in microwave first. Add egg mixture to desired additions and let eggs start to set before stirring. Continue to stir until all eggs are set. If you're in a hurry, transfer mixture to a baking dish and place in a 350 degree oven to set while you're busy doing your rush hour activities. Check and stir about every 5 minutes. It's ready when the eggs are completely set. Sprinkle with Parmesan cheese and crushed red pepper. You can always add a dollop of sour cream for that extra bam!

"Eggs by any name are easy to fix and light to digest,
especially if eating late. Ready in minutes! "

Barbara Allen   Ayala High School, Chino, CA

Grilled Portabello Mushrooms

Serves 4

8 (large) Portabello mushrooms
virgin olive oil
garlic powder
onion powder
cayenne pepper
paprika
salt and pepper

Clean and stem mushrooms. With the bottoms up in a shallow pan, add dry ingredients to taste and cover entire mushroom with olive oil. I usually let mushrooms soak up all the oil before I turn it to season the other side. Let mushrooms marinate for at least 1 hour. Grill each side about 5 to 7 minutes (depending on how large and thick mushrooms are) grilling bottom side down first. Serve immediately.

Stephanie San Sebastian   Central High School, Fresno, CA

Insalata Pizzas

Serves 4

4 (7") pitas
2 teaspoons bottled garlic, minced
1 cup mozzarella cheese, shredded (4 ounces)
$1/2$ cup Vidalia or other sweet onion, thinly sliced
1 tablespoon cider vinegar
2 teaspoons extra virgin olive oil
$1/4$ teaspoon crushed red pepper
1 cup grape tomatoes
$1/4$ cup Kalamata olives, pitted, coarsely chopped
2 tablespoons fresh basil leaves, chopped
4 cups packaged gourmet salad greens

Preheat oven to 475 degrees. Place pitas on baking sheet. Spread $1/2$ teaspoon garlic on each pita. Sprinkle each with $1/4$ cup cheese and divide onion evenly among pitas. Bake 8 minutes or until edges are browned and cheese is bubbly. While pitas bake, combine vinegar, oil and pepper in a large bowl, stirring with a whisk. Stir in tomatoes, olives and basil. Add salad greens and toss gently to coat. Place 1 pita on each of 4 plates. Top each with 1 cup salad and serve immediately.

"Keep pita and flatbread handy for a quick pizza crust,
sandwiches, or baked for chips. Very versatile."

Sue Hope   Lompoc High School, Lompoc, CA

Manicotti
Serves 5 - 6

1 $1/_2$ cups ricotta cheese
1 egg, beaten
1 teaspoon parsley, chopped
$3/_4$ cup Mozzarella cheese, shredded
5 to 6 manicotti shells, uncooked
Sauce:
2 (8 ounce) cans tomato sauce
1 teaspoon parsley, chopped
1 teaspoon basil
1 teaspoon oregano
1 clove garlic, minced
salt and pepper, to taste
water
2 teaspoons Parmesan cheese, grated

Preheat oven to 350 degrees. Combine ricotta, egg, 1 teaspoon parsley, and Mozzarella until well mixed. Using a teaspoon, gently fill each shell until all mixture is gone. Be careful not to break the shells. Place in an 8" x 8" pan. Prepare sauce: Mix together tomato sauce, remaining 1 teaspoon parsley, basil, oregano and garlic. Salt and pepper to taste. Pour over shells. Add enough water so sauce covers the shells. Sprinkle with Parmesan cheese. Cover pan with foil (shiny side down) and place in oven for 1 hour or until shells are tender.

"The students in our foods classes enjoy this recipe!
The filling can be made head of time."

Bonnie Landin   Garden Grove High School, Garden Grove, CA

Mini Pizza
Serves 4

1 (large) onion, coarsely chopped
1 tablespoon olive oil
1 (12 ounce) jar roasted red peppers, patted dry, chopped
salt and pepper, to taste
4 (7") tortillas
$1/_2$ cup cheese (pepper jack, mozzarella,
    or whatever is on hand), shredded

Preheat oven to 475 degrees. Cook onion in oil over medium heat, about 5 minutes. Stir in peppers, salt and pepper to taste. Toast tortillas on burner (electric or gas) over low heat, turning once, until slightly puffed and browned in spots, about 30 seconds on each side. Arrange tortillas in 1 layer on baking sheet. Spoon one fourth of the onion mixture onto each tortilla.

Sprinkle pizzas with cheese and bake until cheese is melted and edges of tortillas are browned, about 5 minutes.

"You can use whatever ingredients you have on hand. Pitas split in half lengthwise and baked for about 5 minutes before putting on the toppings work about the same. I use a similar recipe with toasted English muffins. It's a student favorite!"

Susan Sullins   Central Middle School, Oroville, CA

Papa Pucci's Primavera

Serves 2

$1/4$ cup olive oil
1 clove garlic, minced
1 zucchini, sliced
1 summer squash, sliced
1 pound mushrooms
2 tomatoes, diced
salt and pepper, to taste
$1/2$ pound spaghetti
water, to boil
1 box peas, frozen
freshly grated Parmesan cheese

In large skillet, heat oil over medium heat and sauté garlic. Add squash; sauté until soft and transparent. stir in mushroom and cook 2 minutes. Add tomatoes and cook 1 minute more; remove from heat, salt and pepper to taste and set aside. Meanwhile, bring water to a boil. Add spaghetti and peas and cook until pasta is al dente. Drain and add to vegetable mixture. Toss until well coated. Top with Parmesan cheese.

"This is a healthy blend of flavors and one of my all time favorite recipes. Especially great in the summertime!!"

Alicia Pucci   Kenilworth Junior High School, Petaluma, CA

Pasta, Beans & Greens
Serves 4

1 tablespoon oil
$^1/_2$ cup onion, chopped
$^1/_2$ cup carrot, grated
1 clove garlic, minced
$^1/_2$ teaspoon dried oregano
$^1/_2$ teaspoon salt
$^1/_4$ teaspoon black pepper
1 can (lowfat/low sodium) chicken or vegetable broth
1 (14.5 ounce) can Italian-style diced tomatoes, undrained
$^1/_2$ cup penne pasta, uncooked
1 (16 once) can white beans, rinsed and drained
$^1/_2$ package frozen chopped spinach,
   (thawed, drained, squeezed of all liquid)
$^1/_4$ cup Parmesan cheese, grated

Heat oil in a medium sauce pan. Add onion, carrot and garlic and sauté 5 minutes. add oregano, salt, pepper, broth and tomatoes with liquid. Bring to a boil. Cover, reduce heat and simmer 10 minutes. Increase heat to medium-high. Add pasta, beans and spinach; cook 10 to 14 minutes or until pasta is done, stirring occasionally. Sprinkle each serving with grated Parmesan cheese.

"This is a quick and hearty vegetarian dish from Cooking Light magazine."
Debbie Powers   Griffiths Middle School, Downey, CA

Pasta Primavera
Serves 8

6 ounces dried fettuccini
3 tablespoons butter, divided
2 cups fresh broccoli florets
1 cup carrots, bias-sliced (2 medium)
1 (medium) onion, cut into wedges
1 clove garlic, minced
1 cup pea pods
$^1/_4$ cup cashews, coarsely chopped
$^1/_4$ cup chicken broth
1 teaspoon thyme
$^1/_4$ teaspoon pepper
$^1/_4$ cup Parmesan cheese, grated

Cook fettuccini 8 to 10 minutes; drain. In a large skillet, melt 2 tablespoons butter. Stir in broccoli, carrots, onion and garlic. Cook and stir over medium heat about 3 minutes. Stir in pea pods. Cook 2 minutes. Stir in cooked fettuccini, the remaining 1 tablespoon butter, cashews, broth, thyme and pepper. Cover and cook 1 minute more. Sprinkle with Parmesan cheese and serve.

"This is one of my husbands favorite dishes."

Charlotte Runyan   Saddleback High School, Santa Ana, CA

Pasta Romanesco
Serves 2-3

    8 ounces bow tie or penne pasta
    7 ounces roasted red peppers ($1/2$ of a 14-ounce jar), rinsed
    $1/2$ teaspoon Tabasco sauce
    1 (14.5 ounce) can chunky tomatoes, drained a bit
    4 ounces mozzarella, cut into little cubes
    3 tablespoons Parmesan cheese, grated

Cook pasta according to package directions. While this is cooking, process the peppers with Tabasco in a food processor until smooth. Scrape into a glass bowl. Add the tomatoes and both cheeses. Microwave until hot, 2 to 3 minutes. Toss with hot, drained pasta and enjoy!

"This has a great unexpected flavor. In the time it takes to cook the pasta, you can also steam your favorite vegetable or add what you like to packaged salad greens."

Margo Olsen   Amador Valley High School, Pleasanton, CA

Pasta Supreme

    1 teaspoon salt
    2 tablespoons + 1 teaspoon olive oil, divided
    2 cups egg noodles
    $1/4$ cup onion, chopped
    1 clove garlic, minced
    $1/2$ teaspoon basil
    1 cup carrots, sliced
    1 cup broccoli, cut into spears
    1 to 3 mushrooms, sliced
    salt and pepper, to taste
    $1/3$ cup Italian salad dressing
    $1/4$ cup Parmesan cheese, grated

Bring 5 to 6 cups water to a boil. Add 1 teaspoon salt and 1 teaspoon oil. Slowly stir in noodles. Cook 8 to 10 minutes until noodles are tender. Drain in colander. Do not rinse noodles as you will lose water soluble vitamins. While noodles are cooking, pour 2 tablespoons olive oil into a skillet and heat. Add onions and garlic and sauté over medium heat for about 2 minutes. Add carrots and stir fry 3 to 5 minutes. Add broccoli and stir fry 2 to 3 minutes. Add mushrooms and cook 2 to 3 minutes more. Season to taste with salt and pepper. Combine noodles and vegetables. Pour in dressing and stir to coat vegetables and noodles. Serve, sprinkled with Parmesan cheese.

"Students and teenagers love this!"

Anne Hawes   Cottonwood High School, Murray, UT

Rice Frittata

Serves 4

$1/2$ cup onion, finely chopped
1 tablespoon butter
8 eggs
$1/2$ cup milk
1 teaspoon salt
1 teaspoon Worcestershire sauce
4 to 5 drops Tabasco sauce
2 cups rice, cooked
1 (6 ounce) can chiles, chopped, undrained
1 (medium) tomato, chopped
$1/2$ cup cheddar cheese, shredded

In a 10" skillet, over medium-high heat, cook onions in butter until tender. Beat eggs with milk and seasonings. Stir in rice, chiles and tomato. Pour into pan. Reduce heat to medium-low. Cover and cook until top is almost set, about 12 to 15 minutes. Sprinkle with cheese. Cover, remove from heat. Let stand about 10 minutes before serving.

"You can add shredded carrot or zucchini for an extra vegetable boost.
Top with salsa when serving."

Jackie Williams   Prospect High School, Saratoga, CA

Supper Spuds

Serves 4

4 (large) russet potatoes
3 tablespoons butter
$1/4$ cup cheddar cheese, grated
3 tablespoons green onion, chopped
4 (large) eggs
Optional: 4 slices bacon, cooked, crumbled

Bake potatoes (conventional or microwave). Scoop out insides. Mix potato with butter, cheese, green onion (and bacon, if using). Re-stuff potato skins with mixture. Make a well in center of each stuffed potato skin. Crack egg into well. Bake at 350 degrees for 15 minutes or until egg is set.

"Great as a meatless entrée!"

Nanci Burkhart   Hueneme High School, Oxnard, CA

Tangy Citrus Vegetarian Wonder

Serves 4

Couscous (whole wheat adds more nutrition)
1 tablespoon olive oil
1 onion, diced
2 garlic cloves, minced
Colorful vegetables of your choice, sliced (leafy greens,
    such as kale or chard, zucchini, or eggplant work well)
Meatless chicken pieces (frozen product made by Quorn)
1 to 2 tomatoes, chopped (optional)
Mojito Sauce from Trader Joe's

Boil water for couscous and follow preparation directions on box. Allow couscous to sit covered, then fluff before serving. Meanwhile, sauté onion until soft and translucent, add garlic, sautéing an additional 2 minutes. Add meatless chicken pieces (a small handful for each diner), sliced vegetables (denser vegetables earlier, tender vegetables later) until al dente. Add chopped tomatoes, if desired, and Mojito sauce, heating until piping hot. Serve over couscous.

"Meals with fresh, sliced, sautéed vegetables are always are a snap to prepare. If the carbohydrate is whole grain and the veggies are dark in color, then the meal is much more nutritionally rich, as well as yummy. Quorn products are found in the frozen food sections of natural foods stores, look for a bright orange box."

Beth Pool   Sobrato High School, Morgan Hill, CA

Tomatoes & Mushrooms with Eggs

Serves 3 - 4

3 tablespoons butter or margarine
1 (small) onion, chopped
1 pound mushrooms, sliced or
    2 (4 ounce) cans sliced mushrooms, drained
2 (28 ounces) cans diced tomatoes, drained
6 to 8 eggs
salt and pepper
1 cup Monterey Jack or cheddar cheese, shredded
1 tablespoon fresh parsley, chopped or 1 teaspoon dried parsley
6 to 8 thick slices Italian bread, toasted

In a large skillet, over medium heat, melt butter or margarine. Add onion and mushrooms; cook, stirring until soft and juices have evaporated. Add tomatoes and stir to heat through. With a spoon, make 6 to 8 well spaces in tomato mixture. Break an egg into each well. Sprinkle with salt and pepper; cover evenly with cheese. Reduce heat to low. Cover and cook until eggs are desired firmness. Top with parsley. Serve over toasted slices of Italian bread.

"My advanced foods class found this recipe and tried it when we were studying about eggs. It would also make a great brunch recipe."

Elaine Dennis   Los Baños High School, Los Baños, CA

Vegetables and Side Dishes

Baked Pineapple

Serves 4 - 6

> 3 cans crushed pineapple
> 3 eggs
> $1/2$ cup sugar
> $1/2$ teaspoon salt
> 8 to 10 slices bread, torn into pieces
> $1/2$ cup margarine or butter, melted

Preheat oven to 350 degrees. Stir together pineapple, eggs, sugar and salt; pour into a greased 9" x 13" pan. In a large glass bowl, melt margarine in microwave (40 to 60 seconds on high). Tear bread into pieces and add to margarine or butter and stir well. Spoon mixture on top of pineapple mixture and bake 30 minutes.

"This is a family recipe passed down from generations.
No holiday is celebrated without this!"

Cyndi Matthews   Etiwanda High School, Etiwanda, CA

Corn Pudding

Serves 8

> 1 (15 ounce) can whole kernel corn
> 1 (15 ounce) can cream style corn
> 1 (8 ounce) container sour cream
> $1/2$ cup (1 cube) butter, melted
> 1 box Jiffy corn bread

Preheat oven to 350 degrees. Mix all ingredients together. Pour into a greased 2-quart casserole baking dish. Bake 1 hour.

"This recipe was given to me by Merkie Pederson after she brought it to a
potluck meal. Very easy and delicious! It also doubles as bread for the meal."

Peg Ellington   Yucca Valley High School, Yucca Valley, CA

Creamy Microwave Macaroni & Cheese
Serves 4

>   4 cups water
>   1 cup elbow macaroni, uncooked
>   2 tablespoons butter
>   3 tablespoons flour
> $1/2$ teaspoon salt
>   1 cup milk
>   1 cup cheddar cheese, grated
>   paprika, bread crumbs (optional)

In a medium saucepan, boil water. Add macaroni and cook 8 minutes; drain. In a glass or microwave safe dish, melt butter for 30 seconds. Blend in flour and salt. Stir in milk until smooth. Microwave 2 minutes, stirring with a fork after 1 minute, until thickened. Stir in cheese until completely melted. Pour well drained macaroni into cheese sauce, mixing well. Microwave at medium-high heat for 3 minutes. If desired, sprinkle top with paprika or bread crumbs, before serving.

Cheryl Whittington   Saddleback High School, Santa Ana, CA

Fried Rice in a Flash
Serves 4-6

>   3 cups rice, cooked
>   2 tablespoons. vegetable oil
>   1 teaspoon sesame oil
>   3 to 4 tablespoons. soy sauce
>   4 slices bacon, cooked and crumbled
>   3 eggs, scrambled
>   4 green onions, chopped
>   1 tablespoon sesame seeds, toasted (optional)

Heat vegetable oil and sesame oil in wok or large skillet over medium-high heat. Add cooked rice and stir until rice is coated and heated through. Stir in soy sauce, then bacon, eggs, and green onions. Garnish with toasted sesame seeds, if desired.

"I often cook extra rice for one meal and use the leftover cooked rice to make this recipe. (Instant) brown rice is a nice whole grain choice. Leftover pieces of chicken, ham or pork are a good addition for a main dish."

Laura de la Motte   Turlock High School, Turlock, CA

Garlic Fries
Serves 6

3 pounds baking potatoes, peeled, cut into $1/4$" thick strips
4 teaspoons vegetable oil
$3/4$ teaspoon salt
nonstick cooking spray
2 tablespoons butter
8 cloves garlic, minced (about 5 teaspoons)
2 tablespoons fresh parsley, finely chopped
2 tablespoons Parmesan cheese, freshly grated

Preheat oven to 400 degrees. Combine first 3 ingredients in a large ziploc bag, tossing to coat. Arrange potatoes in a single layer on a baking sheet that has been sprayed with nonstick cooking spray. Bake 50 minutes or until potatoes are tender and golden brown, turning after 20 minutes. Place butter and garlic in a large nonstick skillet and cook over low heat 2 minutes, stirring constantly. Add potatoes, parsley, and cheese to pan and toss to coat. Serve immediately.

"Tossing the fries in butter and garlic after cooking makes them unbelievably rich."
Jeri Lundy   Grossmont High School, La Mesa, CA

Herbed Carrots
Serves 4

3 cups baby carrots
3 tablespoon white vinegar
1 tablespoon extra virgin olive oil
1 teaspoon dried oregano
1 teaspoon salt
$1/2$ teaspoon ground black pepper
1 clove garlic, minced

Cook baby carrots in water for 5 minutes or until tender-crisp; drain well. Rinse with cold water; drain. Combine vinegar, oil, oregano, salt, black pepper and garlic; drizzle over carrots. Cover and chill until ready to serve.

"Quick, cold side dish to have handy.
Also good when served warm or with a crudite platter."
Sue Hope   Lompoc High School, Lompoc, CA

Microwave Potatoes

Serves 3 to 4

12 to 15 (small) red or white potatoes or a mixture of both
2 tablespoons butter
$1/_8$ teaspoon black pepper
2 teaspoons powdered dry ranch dressing
2 teaspoons fresh chopped chives

Wash potatoes and pat dry. Cut potatoes into 1" pieces for even cooking. Place potatoes in microwave-safe casserole dish. Add butter and pepper. Microwave potatoes on high 6 to 8 minutes, until tender. Sprinkle potatoes with Ranch Dressing mix and chives. Cool slightly and serve.

Suzi Schneider   Bret Harte High School, Angles Camp, CA

"More Please" Broccoli & Rice

Serves 4 - 6

1 (10 ounce) package frozen broccoli
1 cup quick-cooking rice, uncooked
1 cup water
1 cup cheddar cheese, shredded

In medium saucepan, combine frozen broccoli, rice and water. Bring to a boil, stirring occasionally to break up broccoli. Remove from heat. Cover and let stand 5 minutes. Return pan to cook on low heat and stir in cheese until melted.

"If kids like broccoli already, it'll disappear even faster.
I found this in a Fast-Fixin' Kids Recipes book."

Paula Skrifvars   Brea Junior High School, Brea, CA

Oven Roasted Potatoes & Vegetables

Serves 6

2 $1/_2$ cups refrigerated new potato wedges (from 20 ounce bag)
1 (medium) red bell pepper, cut into 1" pieces
1 (small) zucchini, cut into $1/_2$" pieces
4 ounces fresh mushrooms, quartered (to make 1 cup)
2 teaspoons olive oil
$1/_2$ teaspoon dried Italian seasoning
$1/_4$ teaspoon garlic salt
non-stick cooking spray

Heat oven to 450 degrees. Spray 15" x 10" x 1" pan with nonstick cooking spray. In large bowl, toss all ingredients to coat. Spread evenly in pan. Bake 15 to 20 minutes, stirring once halfway through baking time, until vegetables are tender and lightly browned.

Shirley Marshman   West Middle School, Downey, CA

Roasted Asparagus

Serves 4

1 1/2 pounds asparagus, fresh
2 teaspoons olive oil
2 tablespoons chervil or 2 teaspoons tarragon
coarse salt

Preheat oven to 475 degrees. Clean and snap off bottoms of asparagus. Combine oil and herbs. Place asparagus in a greased 15" x 10" x 1" pan. Drizzle oil and herb mixture over asparagus. Sprinkle lightly with salt. Roast, uncovered, in oven for 6 to 8 minutes.

"Easy and healthy way to fix fresh asparagus...delicious!"

Chrisann Boone   Reedley High School, Reedley, CA

Seasoned Red Potatoes

Serves 8

2 pounds (small) red potatoes
2 tablespoons olive oil
2 tablespoons butter
2 tablespoons thyme
salt and pepper, to taste

Preheat oven to 350 degrees. Wash and quarter potatoes. Microwave on high 4 to 6 minutes. Drizzle with olive oil. Toss with butter. Bake in oven 20 minutes. Toss potatoes with thyme. Season with salt and pepper and serve.

April Rosendahl   Chino High School, Chino, CA

Tasty Baked Beans

Serves 12-15

Crockpot
RECIPE!

2 (28 ounce) cans Bush's Baked Beans
1 (15 ounce) can whole cranberry sauce
1/4 cup onion, minced or 1 (large) onion chopped

Combine ingredients in a crockpot and cook on low 2 to 3 hours. Note: These beans may be cooked up to 10 hours in crockpot on low setting. They can also be baked in the oven for 2 hours at 325 degrees.

Sue Waterbury   San Luis Obispo High School, San Luis Obispo, CA

Zucchini Bake

Serves 6

1 1/2 pounds zucchini, cut into small pieces
nonstick cooking spray
1 cup cheese, shredded
1 can onion rings
2 eggs, beaten
1 tablespoon butter

Preheat oven to 350 degrees. Cook zucchini in microwave until somewhat tender. Place in bottom of a 9" x 13" baking dish that has been sprayed with nonstick cooking spray. Mix cheese with onion rings and eggs and pour over zucchini. Dot with butter and bake 25 to 35 minutes.

"Easy and delicious."

Teresa Watson   Don Juan Avila Middle School, Aliso Viejo, CA

Zucchini Casserole

Serves 6-8

1 package Stove Top stuffing (Chicken)
2 to 3 cups zucchini, sliced about 1/4" thick
1 can cream of chicken soup

Preheat oven to 350 degrees. Make stove top stuffing according to package directions and spread evenly over the bottom of a baking dish. Boil zucchini just until tender; drain and place on top of the stuffing mixture. Slightly thin one can of cream of chicken soup and pour over zucchini. Place in oven and warm through, about 10 minutes.

"This will make zucchini everyone's favorite vegetable!"

Linda A. Stokes   Riverton High School, Riverton, UT

Chocolate & Vanilla Swirled Cheese Pie

Serves 8

2 (8 ounce) packages cream cheese, softened
$1/2$ cup sugar
1 teaspoon vanilla
2 eggs
1 (9 ounce) extra serving size packaged crumb crust
1 cup Hershey's Special Dark® chocolate chips
$1/4$ cup milk
red raspberry jam (optional)

Preheat oven to 350 degrees. Beat cream cheese, sugar and vanilla in mixer bowl until well blended. Add eggs; mix thoroughly. Spread 2 cups batter in crumb crust. Place chocolate chips in medium microwave-safe bowl. Microwave on high 1 minute; stir. If necessary, microwave an additional 15 seconds at a time, stirring after each heating, until chocolate is melted and smooth when stirred. Cool slightly. Add chocolate and milk to remaining batter; blend thoroughly. Drop chocolate batter by tablespoonfuls onto vanilla batter. Gently swirl with knife for marbled effect. Bake 30 to 45 minutes or until center is almost set. Cool; refrigerate several hours or overnight. Drizzle with warmed red raspberry jam, if desired. Cover; refrigerate leftovers.

Hershey Foods, Inc.   www.hersheys.com

No Baking!

No-Bake Chocolate & Peanut Butter Cookies

Makes 2 dozen

1 $1/_2$ cups Hershey's semisweet chocolate chips, divided

2 tablespoons shortening, divided (do not use butter or margarine)

1 (10 ounce) package Reese's peanut butter chips, divided

2 $1/_2$ cups (5 ounce can) chow mein noodles, coarsely broken, divided

$1/_2$ cup quick-cooking rolled oats, divided

dried apricots, cut into small pieces (optional).

Cover tray with waxed paper. Place 1 cup chocolate chips and 1 tablespoon shortening in medium microwave-safe bowl. Microwave on high 1 to 1 $1/_2$ minutes or until chips are melted when stirred; stir in 1 $1/_4$ cups chow mein noodles and $1/_4$ cup oats. Drop by heaping teaspoons onto prepared tray; flatten slightly. Press $2/_3$ cup peanut butter chips into cookies; allow to set until firm. Place remaining 1 cup peanut butter chips and remaining 1 tablespoon shortening in another medium microwave-safe bowl. Microwave on high 1 to 2 minutes or until chips are melted when stirred; stir in remaining 1 $1/_4$ cups chow mein noodles and remaining $1/_4$ cup oats. Drop and flatten as directed above. Press $1/_2$ cup chocolate chips into cookies; allow to set until firm. Garnish with apricots, if desired.

Hershey Foods, Inc.   **www.hersheys.com**

Cakes Cookies and Desserts

1-2-3 Peanut Butter Cookies
Makes 12 - 16

1 $1/3$ cup granulated sugar, divided
1 egg
1 cup peanut butter, firmly packed

Preheat oven to 350 degrees. In medium-sized bowl, place 1 cup sugar, egg and peanut butter. Using a wooden spoon, stir until thoroughly blended and smooth. Take a spoonful of dough and roll into a ball about 1" round. In a small bowl, pour remaining $1/3$ cup sugar. Dip the ball into sugar to coat evenly and place on ungreased cookie sheet. Using a fork, flatten into a criss-cross pattern. Repeat with remaining dough. Bake 10 to 13 minutes. Note: Cookies will be very soft when you remove them from the oven. Cool completely before removing them from the cookie sheet.

"Our cafeteria manager, Doreen Ponce,
heard this recipe on the radio and shared it with me."

Marianne Traw   Ball Junior High School, Anaheim, CA

10-Minute Peanut Brittle
Serves 6

1 cup sugar
$1/2$ cup light corn syrup
$1/8$ teaspoon salt
1 $1/2$ cups roasted peanuts
1 tablespoon margarine
1 teaspoon vanilla
1 teaspoon baking soda

In a 2 quart microwave casserole dish, combine sugar, corn syrup and salt. Microwave on high 5 minutes. Stir in peanuts. Microwave 3 to 5 minutes, stirring after 3 minutes, until syrup and peanuts are lightly browned. Stir in margarine, vanilla and soda until light and foamy. Spread to $1/4$" thickness on a well-buttered cookie sheet. When cool, break into pieces.

"This is a great recipe for candy making.
It is much better than the range method."

Carol Drescher   Oxnard High School, Oxnard, CA

4-Minute Brownie Pie

Serves 8

2 eggs
1 cup sugar
pinch salt
$1/2$ cup butter or margarine, softened
$1/2$ cup flour
4 tablespoons cocoa
1 teaspoon vanilla
$1/2$ cup nuts, chopped

Preheat oven to 325 degrees. Place eggs, sugar, salt, butter, flour, cocoa and vanilla in a small mixing bowl. Beat until smooth. Stir in nuts. Pour into greased 9" pie pan. Bake 30 minutes.

"It's great to serve warm with vanilla ice cream
and all of your favorite toppings."

Dotti Jones   Etiwanda High School, Etiwanda, CA

Angel Coconut Lush
Serves 10

1 (4 serving size) package Jell-O vanilla instant pudding
1 (20 ounce) can crushed pineapple, in juice, undrained
1 cup coconut,flaked
1 cup Cool Whip, thawed
1 (10 ounce) round angel food cake, prepared
6 fresh strawberries or kiwi, sliced

Mix dry pudding mix with pineapple and juice. Stir in coconut and gently fold in Cool Whip. Cut cake horizontally into 3 layers. Place bottom cake layer, cut side, up, on serving plate. Spread $1/3$ of the pudding mixture onto cake layer; cover with middle layer and repeat, ending with last third of topping. Decorate top with fresh strawberries or kiwi (or both!).

"This recipe is dedicated to an outstanding individual who is a role model to all who know him. Besides being a coconut lover, he gives freely to students to improve their self-esteem and encourage their strengths to enable them to go on to college. He is also a heck of a lot of fun to be with. Thanks, Kent - you are amazing!"

Brenda Burke   Mt. Whitney High School, Visalia, CA

Apple Bread Pudding
Serves 6

3 cups dry bread cubes (4 slices bread)
1 $1/2$ cups applesauce
$1/8$ teaspoon cinnamon
dash nutmeg
2 tablespoons butter
2 eggs, beaten
2 cups milk
$1/2$ cup sugar
$1/2$ teaspoon vanilla
dash salt
ground cinnamon

Preheat oven to 350 degrees. In a buttered 8" x 8" x 2" baking pan, layer half the dry bread cubes. In another dish, combine applesauce with $1/8$ teaspoon cinnamon and nutmeg. Spread over bread cubes. Layer remaining bread cubes atop. Dot with butter. Combine egg, milk, sugar, vanilla and salt. Pour over bread mixture. Lightly sprinkle cinnamon over top. Bake 55 to 60 minutes, until a knife inserted just off center comes out clean.

"The new world had no apple trees, so when the pilgrims arrived in New England, they lost no time in starting trees from seed. Apple orchards became so valuable that by 1648, Governor John Endicott traded 500 apples trees for 250 acres of land."

Linnea Howe   Pacifica High School, Oxnard, CA

Boater's Flan

Serves 6

    1 jar caramel ice cream topping
    3 eggs
    1 can sweetened condensed milk
    1 can evaporated milk
    1 tablespoon vanilla

Put about 1 tablespoon caramel sauce in the bottom of each custard cup. In a medium bowl, beat eggs with whisk. Gradually whisk in the sweetened condensed milk, then the evaporated milk and vanilla. Pour into the custard cups. Set cups in a water bath and bake at 350 degrees for 45 minutes or until a dinner knife inserted into the center comes out clean. Serve warm or cold.

"I used to bake this on board our sailboat.
This takes 5 minutes to prepare and while it's baking you can entertain guests
and cook the rest of your meal. By the time you've finished eating
and the dishes are done and the coffee's ready, the flan is ready to serve."
Sandra Massey   Mt. View High School, El Monte, CA

Cake Mix Cookies

Makes 30

    1 box cake mix, any flavor
    2 eggs
    $1/_2$ cup oil
    2 tablespoons water
    small bowl of sugar

Preheat oven to 350 degrees. Combine cake mix with eggs, oil and water in a large bowl. Shape dough into walnut-sized balls and roll in sugar. Place onto cookie sheet and flatten slightly with bottom of a glass. Bake 10 to 12 minutes. Cool on wire cooking rack.

"Try adding chocolate chips, chopped nuts or dried fruit."
Joye Cantrell   Rialto High School, Rialto, CA

Cherry Cheesecake

Serves 6

1 (8 ounce) package cream cheese, room temperature
1 can sweetened condensed milk
$1/3$ cup lemon juice
1 prepared graham cracker crust
1 can cherry pie filling

Beat cream cheese with sweetened condensed milk until smooth. Add lemon juice and mix well. Pour into prepared crust. Top with cherry pie filling. Chill.

"This has been a quick favorite recipe that I have been making since I was a teenager."

Celeste Giron   Riverton High School, Riverton, UT

Chocolate Almond Torte

Makes 16 pieces

1 $1/2$ cups sugar
$3/4$ cup butter, melted
2 eggs
1 teaspoon almond extract
1 $1/2$ teaspoons vanilla extract
$1/2$ teaspoon salt
1 $1/2$ cups flour
$1/2$ cup chocolate chips
$1/2$ cup sliced almonds
1 tablespoon granulated sugar

Preheat oven to 350 degrees. Blend sugar and melted butter together in a medium size mixing bowl. Beat in eggs. Stir in extracts. Stir in salt and flour mixing until well blended. Spread batter in a greased 9" round cake pan. Sprinkle batter with chocolate chips, then almonds, and finally the sugar. Press lightly with the fingers to push toppings into the batter a little way. Bake 30 to 35 minutes until golden brown. Allow to cool before cutting into 16 wedges.

"This dessert tastes great day old as well as fresh from the oven."

Linda Falkenstien   Morro Bay High School, Morro Bay, CA

Chocolate & Vanilla Swirled Cheesepie

Serves 8 (Photo opposite page 128)

2 (8 ounce) packages cream cheese, softened
$1/2$ cup sugar
1 teaspoon vanilla
2 eggs
1 (9 ounce) extra serving size packaged crumb crust
1 cup Hershey's Special Dark chocolate chips
$1/4$ cup milk
red raspberry jam (optional)

Preheat oven to 350 degrees. Beat cream cheese, sugar and vanilla in mixer bowl until well blended. Add eggs; mix thoroughly. Spread 2 cups batter in crumb crust. Place chocolate chips in medium microwave-safe bowl. Microwave on high 1 minute; stir. If necessary, microwave an additional 15 seconds at a time, stirring after each heating, until chocolate is melted and smooth when stirred. Cool slightly. Add chocolate and milk to remaining batter; blend thoroughly. Drop chocolate batter by tablespoonfuls onto vanilla batter. Gently swirl with knife for marbled effect. Bake 30 to 45 minutes or until center is almost set. Cool; refrigerate several hours or overnight. Drizzle with warmed red raspberry jam, if desired. Cover; refrigerate leftovers.

Hershey Foods, Inc. www.hersheys.com

Chocolate Caramel Coconut Cookies

Makes 4 dozen

$3/4$ cup coconut, shredded
2 $1/4$ cups flour
1 teaspoon baking soda
$1/2$ teaspoon salt
$1/2$ cup butter, softened
$3/4$ cup granulated sugar
$3/4$ cup brown sugar
1 teaspoon vanilla
2 eggs
1 cup toffee bits
$3/4$ cup chopped semisweet or milk chocolate (or chocolate chips)

Preheat oven to 350 degrees. Toast coconut by spreading it on a parchment paper lined baking sheet and baking in oven for 5 minutes or until lightly golden. Toss the coconut halfway through baking to ensure even browning. Cool completely before adding to cookies. Stir flour, baking soda, and salt together with a whisk. Cream together butter, both sugars, and vanilla until light and fluffy. Beat in eggs one at a time. Gradually stir flour mixture to creamed ingredients. Stir in toffee, chocolate, and coconut. Drop by rounded teaspoonfuls onto parchment lined baking sheets. Space cookies 2" apart. Bake 9 to 11 minutes. Let cookies sit 1 minute on the baking pan before transferring to cooling racks to cool completely. Note: You can just pull the parchment paper onto the cooling rack with all of the cookies on it to save cleanup.

"This cookie recipe is a a favorite of my family and friends. Saver Tip: When you make any drop cookie recipe use a portion scoop to put cookie dough on a lined sheet pan and instead of baking them, freeze the balls of dough on the pan. After they freeze, transfer the dough balls to a plastic bag and label it with the time and temp for baking. Before baking, set the dough out on the pan about 15 minutes to defrost."

Holly Pittman   El Capitan High School, Lakeside, CA

Chocolate Cheesecake Squares
Serves 10 - 12

    1 frozen cheesecake
    1 package chocolate candy melting wafers
    1 package white chocolate candy melting wafers

Cut frozen cheesecake into bite-sized squares. Place on cookie sheet, then place in freezer. Melt chocolate and white chocolate wafers according to package directions separately. Dip cheesecake squares into chocolate one at a time; half in the chocolate and half in the white chocolate. Drizzle squares with opposite chocolate for decoration. Refreeze until ready to serve.

"An easy last minute or do ahead dessert.
The presentation is very festive for a party. Delicious too!"

Teresa Hayes   Buena High School, Ventura, CA

Chunky Mallow Candy
Makes about 2 dozen

    1 (12 ounce) package semi sweet or milk chocolate pieces
    1 cup chunk style peanut butter
    4 cups miniature marshmallows

Melt chocolate pieces with peanut butter in sauce pan over low heat, stirring until smooth. Fold in marshmallows. Pour into greased 9" square pan; chill until firm. Cut into squares.

"I use this as a fun demo for the students.
They are amazed how quickly the candy is ready, and how good it tastes."

Renee Paulsin   Hemet High School, Hemet, CA

Dump Cake (Gumbiner Special)

Serves 16

2 cans cherry pie filling
1 box white cake mix
$1/2$ cup margarine

Preheat oven to 350 degrees. Grease a 9" x 13" pan. Pour both cans of pie filling into pan. Sprinkle dry cake mix over pie filling. Cut margarine into pieces; dot over dry cake mix. Bake about 40 minutes, until golden brown.

"My friend, Cindy, gave me this recipe in high school. I have made it literally hundreds of times! You can use any combination of filling and flavor of cake mix. A favorite is apple pie filling and spice cake! My children choose this over a birthday cake!"

Gaylen Roe   Magnolia Junior High School, Chino, CA

Easy No-Bake Cheesecake

Serves 8

1 (large) package instant vanilla pudding
1 (16 ounce) container sour cream
1 (20 ounce) can crushed pineapple, drained
1 graham cracker crust

Mix together pudding and sour cream. Stir in drained pineapple. Pour into pie crust. Chill and serve.

"This easy little recipe actually tastes close to the real thing. Great for a last-minute dessert and is refreshing and light on a summer evening."

Beckie Bloemker   Foothill High School, Sacramento, CA

English Toffee

Makes about $1/2$ pound

1 cup real butter
1 cup sugar
1 (small) package almonds, sliced, divided
$1/2$ cup chocolate chips

Melt butter slowly in heavy pan. Add sugar and bring to a boil. Stirring constantly with a wooden spoon, add half of the almonds. Continue stirring and cooking until candy reaches hard-crack stage (when mixture changes color). Quickly pour mixture out onto a large lightly buttered cookie sheet and spread out. (Do not scrape pan - soak it immediately). Cool slightly and top with chocolate chips. Spread chips when they become shiny. Top with remaining almonds. After several hours, break into pieces.

"This is a very easy recipe that was originally given to me by Pam Ford, another Home Economics teacher. We prepare this recipe in our Advanced Foods class and the students really enjoy it."

Diane Castro   Temecula Valley High School, Temecula, CA

Fall Apple Dip

Makes 1 1/2 cups

      8 ounces cream cheese
      1 cup brown sugar
      1 teaspoon vanilla

Mix ingredients together; chill. Serve with sliced apples or other fruits of your choice.

"My friend, Dixie Stephens, gave me this recipe."

Dr. Terry Kluever   **Coronado High School, Henderson, NV**

Fruit Cobbler

Serves 8 - 10

      4 cups fruit
      1 cup sugar
      1/2 cup butter
      1 cup flour
      1 cup sugar
      3/4 cup milk
      2 teaspoons baking powder
      dash salt

Preheat oven to 375 degrees. Mix fruit with sugar and set aside. Melt butter in a 9" x 13" pan. In a separate bowl, mix together the remaining ingredients. Pour batter on the melted butter. Spoon the fruit mixture on top. Bake 40 to 45 minutes or until fruit is tender and the dough browned.

"This is so easy and quick and tastes great warm with ice cream or it can be served cold. You can use fresh fruit such as peaches, apples, or apricots. I have used drained canned peaches when fruit is out of season."

Elizabeth Thornburg   **Selma High School, Selma, CA**

Grandma's Easy Pull-Aparts

Serves 4

      1 can ready made pop up regular biscuits (can of 10)
      1 cup butter
      1/2 cup sugar
      1 teaspoon cinnamon

Preheat oven to 350 degrees. Pop open the can biscuits. Cut each biscuits in four pieces. Place butter in an 8 inch round cake pan or 8 inch square pan. Place butter on stove burner and melt the butter on low. Remove from heat. Drop biscuit pieces in butter. Mix them in the butter until well coated on all sides. Mix the sugar and cinnamon in a small bowl. Pour all the sugar, cinnamon mixture on top of biscuits. Mix until the biscuits are well coated. Lightly press the biscuits evenly in the pan. Bake about 20 minutes, until golden brown. Place a plate on top of the pan while still hot. Carefully invert

Allow the the sugar mixture to completely drizzle on the biscuits about 2 minutes before removing the pan. Enjoy while it's warm.

"My students love this quick easy dessert."

Jane Greaves   Central High School West, Fresno, CA

Grandma's Fudge
Makes 3 pounds

$3/4$ cup margarine or butter
3 cups sugar
1 (5 ounce) can evaporated milk
1 $1/2$ packages (8 squares) semisweet baking chocolate, cut up
1 (7 ounce) jar marshmallow creme
1 teaspoon vanilla
1 cup walnuts, chopped (optional)

Microwave margarine or butter in a 4 quart microwavable bowl on high until melted. Add sugar and milk; mix well. Microwave 5 minutes or until mixture begins to boil, stirring after 3 minutes. Stir well, scraping down sides of bowl. Microwave 5 $1/2$ minutes, stirring after 3 minutes. Let stand 2 minutes. Add chopped chocolate and marshmallow creme. Add vanilla and walnuts, if desired. Mix well. Pour immediately into a foil-lined 9" square pan; spread evenly to cover bottom of pan. Cool at room temperature for 4 hours. Cut into 1" squares. Store in airtight container.

"This fudge is quick to make and melts in your mouth.
It does need about 4 hours to set up properly."

Donna Small   Santana High School, Santee, CA

Lemon Chewy Cookies
Makes 3 dozen

1 package lemon cake mix
4.5 to 5 ounces Cool Whip
1 egg
powdered sugar

Preheat oven to 350 degrees. Mix together cake mix, Cool Whip and egg. Drop by spoonfuls into powdered sugar, coating entirely. Bake on ungreased cookie sheet until lightly browned, about 10 minutes.

"Yummy, soft and good. Can be made with any flavor cake mix!"

Sonja Tyree   Ayala High School, Chino Hills, CA

Lemon (No-Bake) Cheesecake

Serves 4 - 6

> 1 prepared graham cracker or cookie crust
> 1 can (14 ounce) Borden sweetened condensed milk
> 12 ounces cream cheese, room temperature
> 1 teaspoon lemon zest
> $1/3$ cup lemon juice
> *Topping:*
> 1 cup sour cream
> 2 tablespoons powdered sugar
> lemon twist for garnish

Remove plastic cover from pie crust. Clean cover and set aside. Place sweetened-condensed milk, cream cheese, and lemon zest in blender; cover and blend. With blender running, slowly pour lemon juice through hole in cover. Continue until well blended. Pour mixture into crust and spread to edges. Place plastic cover over pie and refrigerate at least 2 hours. Mix sour cream and sugar for topping. Remove plastic cover and spread carefully over cold pie. Garnish center with lemon twist. Keep refrigerated until ready to serve.

"Good use of blender appliance and various other kitchen utensils other than making smoothies in the cooking lab."

Sharlene Young   Ysmael Villegas Middle School, Riverside, CA

Lemon Pie in a Blender

Serves 6

> 1 (large) lemon, thoroughly washed
> 4 eggs
> 1 $1/2$ cups sugar
> $1/2$ cup butter
> 1 unbaked pie crust shell

Preheat oven to 350 degrees. Cut off ends of lemon and cut into eighths. Remove seeds. Place cut lemon in blender and pulse until liquefied. Add eggs, sugar and butter and blend until completely mixed. Pour mixture into prepared pie crust and bake 45 to 50 minutes.

"This is my mother's recipe. She never sacrifices quality for convenience. This recipe is quick and easy as well as delicious!"

Deborah Scott-Toux   Eisenhower High School, Rialto, CA

Mini Cheesecakes

Serves 12

2 (8 ounce) packages cream cheese, softened
$1/2$ cup sugar
$1/2$ teaspoon vanilla
2 eggs
12 vanilla wafers
12 muffin liners
Optional Toppings: Shredded coconut, jelly beans, shoestring licorice

Preheat oven to 350 degrees. Using a mixer, beat cream cheese with sugar and vanilla. Add eggs, one at a time, beating just until blended. Place a vanilla wafer in bottom of each muffin liner in muffin pan. Divide mixture evenly into each liner. Bake 20 minutes or until centers are almost set. Cool. Refrigerate at least 2 hours. Note: To make Easter baskets, place 1 tablespoon shredded coconut on top of each cheesecake. Place 3 to 4 jelly beans on top of coconut and fashion a handle out of shoestring licorice, pushing down into mini cheesecakes to secure.

"This is so cute for Easter–or just enjoy plain!"

Sheri Rader   Chaparral High School, Las Vegas, NV

Mud Pie

Serves 8-10

$1/2$ package chocolate wafers
$1/2$ cube butter, melted
1 quart coffee ice cream, softened
1 $1/2$ cups fudge sauce, room temperature
whipped cream

Crush wafers and add melted butter, mix well. Press mixture into a 9" pie plate. Cover with soft coffee ice cream. Put into freezer until ice cream is firm. Top with fudge sauce. Store in the freezer for approximately 10 hours. To serve, slice pie into 8 to 10 portions and serve on a chilled plate topped with whipped cream.

"The fudge spreads easier if it is placed in the freezer for a short time."

Angela Croce   Mira Mesa High School, San Diego, CA

No-Bake Chocolate & Peanut Butter Cookies

Makes 2 dozen (Photo opposite page 129)

1 $1/_2$ cups Hershey's semisweet chocolate chips, divided
2 tablespoons shortening, divided (do not use butter or margarine)
1 (10 ounce) package Reese's peanut butter chips, divided
2 $1/_2$ cups (5 ounce can) chow mein noodles,
    coarsely broken, divided
$1/_2$ cup quick-cooking rolled oats, divided
dried apricots, cut into small pieces (optional)

Cover tray with waxed paper. Place 1 cup chocolate chips and 1 tablespoon shortening in medium microwave-safe bowl. Microwave on high 1 to 1 $1/_2$ minutes or until chips are melted when stirred; stir in 1 $1/_4$ cups chow mein noodles and $1/_4$ cup oats. Drop by heaping teaspoons onto prepared tray; flatten slightly. Press $2/_3$ cup peanut butter chips into cookies; allow to set until firm. Place remaining 1 cup peanut butter chips and remaining 1 tablespoon shortening in another medium microwave-safe bowl. Microwave on high 1 to 2 minutes or until chips are melted when stirred; stir in remaining 1 $1/_4$ cups chow mein noodles and remaining $1/_4$ cup oats. Drop and flatten as directed above. Press $1/_2$ cup chocolate chips into cookies; allow to set until firm. Garnish with apricots, if desired.

Hershey Foods, Inc. www.hersheys.com

Oh No! I Need Something for Dessert!

Serves 10 - 12

1 (16 ounce) can sliced peaches, with syrup
1 box yellow cake mix
1 stick butter or margarine, melted
1 (8 ounce) container Cool Whip
nonstick cooking spray

Preheat oven to 350 degrees. Spray a 9" x 13" pan with nonstick cooking spray. Spread peaches with syrup over bottom of pan. Sprinkle cake mix evenly over peaches, patting down gently. Drizzle melted butter or margarine over dry mixture. Bake cake 30 to 35 minutes, until golden brown. Serve warm, topped with Cool Whip or ice cream.

"A quick and easy recipe when you need something sweet in a hurry.
Great for unexpected guests."

Janet Policy Ramona High School, Riverside, CA

Orange Crumb Cake

Serves 6

>   1 cup flour
> $1/2$ cup sugar
> $1/4$ cup butter or margarine
>   1 teaspoon cinnamon
>   1 teaspoon baking powder
>   1 egg
> $1/2$ cup orange juice

Lightly grease a 1 quart glass dish or a 9" x 4" dish. Mix flour, sugar and butter or margarine together until mixture is crumbly, like cornmeal. Measure $1/2$ cup of crumbled mixture and put into a second bowl; add 1 teaspoon cinnamon, mix together and set aside. With remaining mixture, stir in baking powder. In a small bowl, beat egg with orange juice. Stir into mixture with baking powder, then fill greased dish, spreading evenly. Sprinkle cinnamon mixture on top and bake in microwave on high for 2 minutes. Turn dish half way through baking. Bake another 2 minutes on high. Test for doneness with a toothpick. Remember just a tad of cooking at a time as mixture will continue to cook upon standing.

"Great to make as a breakfast coffee cake or an after dinner dessert! Quick and delicious!"

Nancy Patten   Placerita Junior High School, Newhall, CA

Peanut Butter Rice Krispy Treats

Makes 24

>   1 cup sugar
>   1 cup corn syrup
>   1 cup peanut butter
>   7 cups crisp rice cereal
> $3/4$ cup milk chocolate chips
> $3/4$ cup butterscotch chips

Combine sugar, corn syrup and peanut butter in saucepan. Melt until smooth. Add crisp rice cereal and stir until coated. Pour into greased oblong pan. Melt chocolate and butterscotch chips together and spread on top. Chill until chocolate is firm.

"My friend, Mary Gordon, shared this tasty recipe with me. It's a great change from the traditional rice krispy treat!"

Debbie Harvey   Amador Valley High School, Pleasanton, CA

Peanut Crispies

Makes 2 ½ dozen

1 (large) bag vanilla baking chips
2 tablespoons peanut butter
1 cup crisp rice cereal
1 cup dry roasted peanuts
1 cup miniature marshmallows

Melt vanilla chips and peanut butter as directed on bag of chips. When melted, stir in cereal and nuts. Let mixture cool slightly, then stir in marshmallows. (If mixture is too hot, marshmallows will melt.) Drop by spoonfuls onto waxed paper and refrigerate until set.

"Thanks to my mom for sharing this super-simple recipe. Be sure to take copies of the recipe with you if you ever take this to a pot luck."

Penny Niadna   Golden West High School, Visalia, CA

Pineapple Cake

Serves 8 - 12

1 yellow cake mix
1 (20 ounce) can crushed pineapple
1 (3 ounce) package instant vanilla pudding mix
½ cup milk
1 (9 ounce) carton Cool Whip
1 cup coconut

Prepare cake according to package directions using a 9" x 13" pan. When done, poke holes all over top. Cool. Pour crushed pineapple, with liquid, over top of cake. Prepare pudding mix with milk. Fold into Cool Whip and spread over top of pineapple. Sprinkle with coconut. Refrigerate overnight.

"This is so easy to make but tastes so elegant, and I don't have to make frosting!"

Monica Blanchette   Landmark Middle School, Moreno Valley, CA

Pineapple Upside Down Cake

Serves 12

$1/4$ cup margarine
$1/2$ to $2/3$ cup light brown sugar
12 slices pineapple (8 ounce and 4 ounce cans, juice reserved)
12 maraschino cherries, rinsed, dried
1 box yellow cake mix
1 cup pineapple juice
$1/2$ cup oil
3 eggs
1 teaspoon vanilla

Preheat oven 350 degrees. Melt margarine and pour into a 9" x 13" inch pan making sure all sides are covered. Add brown sugar evenly to pan. Place pineapple in 4 rows of threes and place a cherry in the center of each one. Mix cake according to the directions on the box using pineapple juice instead of water. Pour over pineapple & brown sugar mixture. Bake until golden brown and cake separates from the sides of the pans, 31 to 35 minutes. Cool for 5 to 10 minutes on a wire rack, shake cake slightly to make sure it is separated from the pan. Place a serving tray or cake board on top & invert cake. If some of the pineapple did not come out of the pan, you can put it in place now. Note: If cake cooks too fast reduce heat to 200 degrees and add additional minutes until the center is done.

"This is a favorite that is sure to get favorable comments."

Jannie Parks   Ramona High School, Riverside, CA

Pudding Pie

Serves 8

1 prepared graham cracker crust
1 large (5.1 ounce) Jell-0 vanilla instant pudding pie filling
    (chocolate also works well)
2 $1/2$ cups milk
Cool Whip

Combine pudding mix and cold milk. Beat in bowl with wire whisk for 2 minutes. Pour pudding mix into prepared graham cracker crust. Let set until firm. Top with desired amount of cool whip.

"This is a favorite dessert wherever it goes."

Liz Aschenbrenner   Sierra High School, Manteca, CA

Quick Apple Crisp

Serves 4 - 6

$1/2$ cup pecans, chopped
1 cup flour
$1/2$ cup butter or margarine
1 cup sugar
2 teaspoons cinnamon
$1/2$ teaspoon nutmeg
$1/2$ cup raisins
1 can apples, sliced
2 teaspoons lemon juice

Preheat oven to 375 degrees. Chop pecans. Sift flour. Cream butter or margarine and sugar; mix in flour, cinnamon, nutmeg, raisins and pecans. Put apples on bottom of 8" x 8" pan. Sprinkle with lemon juice. Spread flour mixture over apples. Bake 30 minutes, until golden brown. Serve warm, with ice cream, if desired.

"You don't have to peel and cut apples so it saves a lot of time. This is my mom's recipe."

Pat Hufnagel   Esperanza High School, Anaheim, CA

Reese's Pieces Cookies

Makes 26 cookies

1 box yellow cake mix, sifted
1 egg
$1/3$ cup water
1 cup peanut butter
Reese's pieces

Preheat oven to 350 degrees. Mix together all ingredients (except Reese's pieces) well. Roll dough into a balls the size of a large walnut or use a cookie dough scoop. Place on cookie sheet Bake 12 to 15 minutes. Remove immediately and press 1 Reese's piece into center of each cookie.

"Children love this easy quick recipe treat!"

Cheryl Moyle   Olympus High School, Salt Lake City, UT

Rum Cake

Serves 8 - 10

$1/2$ cup pecans, chopped
1 package yellow cake mix
1 package instant vanilla pudding
$1/2$ cup dark rum
$1/2$ cup water
$1/2$ cup salad oil
4 eggs
Hot Rum Glaze:
1 cup sugar
$1/2$ cup margarine or butter
$1/4$ cup dark rum
$1/4$ cup water

Preheat oven to 325 degrees. Grease and flour a 10" tube or bundt pan. Sprinkle nuts over bottom. Combine cake mix, pudding mix, rum, water, oil and eggs. Beat 3 to 4 minutes at medium speed. Pour into prepared pan. Bake 50 to 60 minutes. Meanwhile, heat glaze ingredients together in saucepan until melted. Pour hot glaze over hot cake and cool 30 minutes in pan. Invert on plate and serve.

Beverly Ranger   Carpinteria High School, Carpinteria, CA

Toffee Bites

Makes 40

1 stick butter
$1/2$ cup brown sugar
1 teaspoon vanilla
1 cup flour
$1/2$ cup + 3 tablespoons toffee chips (Heath or Skor chips), divided
$1/2$ cup milk chocolate chips

Preheat oven to 350 degrees. In a medium sauce pan over medium heat melt butter. Watch carefully to prevent burning. Remove pan from heat and stir in brown sugar and vanilla. Stir in the flour to make a stiff dough, then stir in $1/2$ cup toffee chips. Spread and pat dough into an ungreased 8" square baking pan. Bake for 20 minutes or until golden brown. Immediately sprinkle with chocolate chips. Wait 1 minute to allow the chocolate to melt, then spread over to make an icing. (If chocolate does not melt, return the pan to the oven for 2 minutes, then spread.) Sprinkle the remaining toffee chips over chocolate. Let the bars cool in the pan for 2 minutes, then use a sharp knife to cut bars into approximately 40 bite size squares. Let cool for 5 minutes more. Refrigerate for 5 to 10 minutes to set the chocolate. Remove bars with a small spatula and serve. Bars can be stored in a tightly covered container for 5 days or freeze up to 2 months

"These are so quick and easy, everyone loves them!"

Leslie Corsini   Nicolas Junior High School, Fullerton, CA

Toffee Popcorn Crunch
Makes 1 1/2 pounds

8 cups popcorn, popped
3/4 cup almonds, whole or slivered
1 1/3 cups (8 ounce package) Heath *Bits 'O Brickle* Toffee Bits
1/2 cup light corn syrup

Preheat oven to 275 degrees. Grease a large roasting pan or two 9" x 13" x 2" baking pans. Place popcorn and almonds in prepared pan(s). Combine toffee bits and corn syrup in heavy medium saucepan. Cook over medium heat, stirring constantly, until toffee is melted, about 12 minutes. Pour over popcorn mixture, stir until evenly coated. Bake 30 minutes, stirring frequently. Remove from oven; stir every 2 minutes until slightly cooled. Cool completely. Store in tightly covered container in cool, dry place. Note: For best results, do not double this recipe.

Hershey Foods, Inc.   **www.hersheys.com**

RushHour RECIPES

Index *of* Contributors

RushHour RECIPES

W

Y

Index of Recipes

RushHour RECIPES

RushHour RECIPES

For additional copies of *this* book, please use the re-order forms below.

For *other* cookbook titles available, please visit our website:

www.californiacookbook.com

RushHour RECIPES

Please send me _____ copy(ies) of *Rush Hour Recipes* at **$10.95** ea. (includes tax and shipping). Make checks payable to **California Cookbook Company**. Mail this form with your check to: **8332 Brush Drive, Huntington Beach, CA 92647**

Enclosed is my check for _____ book(s) at **$10.95** ea $_____.

Name _____

Address _____

City _____ State _____ Zip _____

RushHour RECIPES

Please send me _____ copy(ies) of *Rush Hour Recipes* at **$10.95** ea. (includes tax and shipping). Make checks payable to **California Cookbook Company**. Mail this form with your check to: **8332 Brush Drive, Huntington Beach, CA 92647**

Enclosed is my check for _____ book(s) at **$10.95** ea $_____.

Name _____

Address _____

City _____ State _____ Zip _____

RushHour RECIPES